An Analysis of

# Thomas Paine's

## Rights of Man

Mariana Assis
and
Jason Xidias

www.macat.com
info@macat.com

Cover illustration: Capucine Deslouis

*Cataloguing in Publication Data*
A catalogue record for this book is available from the British Library.
Library of Congress Cataloguing-in-Publication Data is available upon request.

ISBN 978-1-912303-42-7 (hardback)
ISBN 978-1-912128-98-3 (paperback)
ISBN 978-1-912282-30-2 (e-book)

**Notice**
The information in this book is designed to orientate readers of the work under analysis,
to elucidate and contextualise its key ideas and themes, and to aid in the development
of critical thinking skills. It is not meant to be used, nor should it be used, as a
substitute for original thinking or in place of original writing or research. References and
notes are provided for informational purposes and their presence does not constitute
endorsement of the information or opinions therein. This book is presented solely for
educational purposes. It is sold on the understanding that the publisher is not engaged
to provide any scholarly advice. The publisher has made every effort to ensure that
this book is accurate and up-to-date, but makes no warranties or representations with
regard to the completeness or reliability of the information it contains. The information
and the opinions provided herein are not guaranteed or warranted to produce particular
results and may not be suitable for students of every ability. The publisher shall not be
liable for any loss, damage or disruption arising from any errors or omissions, or from
the use of this book, including, but not limited to, special, incidental, consequential or
other damages caused, or alleged to have been caused, directly or indirectly, by the
information contained within.

# CONTENTS

# THE MACAT LIBRARY

The Macat Library is a series of unique academic explorations of seminal works in the humanities and social sciences – books and papers that have had a significant and widely recognised impact on their disciplines. It has been created to serve as much more than just a summary of what lies between the covers of a great book. It illuminates and explores the influences on, ideas of, and impact of that book. Our goal is to offer a learning resource that encourages critical thinking and fosters a better, deeper understanding of important ideas.

Each publication is divided into three Sections: Influences, Ideas, and Impact. Each Section has four Modules. These explore every important facet of the work, and the responses to it.

This Section-Module structure makes a Macat Library book easy to use, but it has another important feature. Because each Macat book is written to the same format, it is possible (and encouraged!) to cross-reference multiple Macat books along the same lines of inquiry or research. This allows the reader to open up interesting interdisciplinary pathways.

To further aid your reading, lists of glossary terms and people mentioned are included at the end of this book (these are indicated by an asterisk [*] throughout) – as well as a list of works cited.

Macat has worked with the University of Cambridge to identify the elements of critical thinking and understand the ways in which six different skills combine to enable effective thinking.
Three allow us to fully understand a problem; three more give us the tools to solve it. Together, these six skills make up the **PACIER** model of critical thinking. They are:

**ANALYSIS** – understanding how an argument is built
**EVALUATION** – exploring the strengths and weaknesses of an argument
**INTERPRETATION** – understanding issues of meaning

**CREATIVE THINKING** – coming up with new ideas and fresh connections
**PROBLEM-SOLVING** – producing strong solutions
**REASONING** – creating strong arguments

To find out more, visit **WWW.MACAT.COM.**

## CRITICAL THINKING AND *RIGHTS OF MAN*

### Primary critical thinking skill: EVALUATION
### Secondary critical thinking skill: REASONING

Thomas Paine's 1791 *Rights of Man* is an impassioned political tract showing how the critical thinking skills of evaluation and reasoning can, and must, be applied to contentious issues.

Divided into two parts, *Rights of Man* is, first, a response to Edmund Burke's arguments against the French Revolution, put forward in his *Reflections on the Revolution in France* – also available in the Macat Library – and, second, an argument for how to run a fair and just society. The first part is a sustained performance in evaluation: Paine takes Burke's arguments, and systematically exposes the ways in which Burke's reasons against revolution are inadequate compared to the necessity of having a just society run according to a universal notion of people's rights as individuals. The second part turns to an examination of different political systems, setting out a powerfully-structured argument for universal rights, a clear constitution enshrined in law, and a universal right to vote.

Though Paine is in many ways a stronger rhetorician than he is a clear thinker, his reasons for preferring democracy to hereditary forms of government are compelling, coherent and clear. *Rights of Man* is a masterclass in how to use good reasoning to present a persuasive argument.

## ABOUT THE AUTHOR OF THE ORIGINAL WORK

Born in Britain in 1737, **Thomas Paine** had a humble, religious upbringing and very little formal education. The course of his life turned in 1774, when he met the great American statesman Benjamin Franklin in London. With Franklin's help, Paine emigrated to the American colonies, where his political writings such as Common Sense contributed to the discontent that resulted in the American Revolution. Paine maintained his stubborn commitment to morality and social justice until his death in 1809 in New Rochelle, New York at the age of 72.

## ABOUT THE AUTHORS OF THE ANALYSIS

**Mariana Assis** is a doctoral candidate at the New School for Social Research, New York.

**Dr Jason Xidias** has held positions at King's College London, the University of California, Berkeley, and the New School of the Humanities.

## ABOUT MACAT

### GREAT WORKS FOR CRITICAL THINKING

Macat is focused on making the ideas of the world's great thinkers accessible and comprehensible to everybody, everywhere, in ways that promote the development of enhanced critical thinking skills.

It works with leading academics from the world's top universities to produce new analyses that focus on the ideas and the impact of the most influential works ever written across a wide variety of academic disciplines. Each of the works that sit at the heart of its growing library is an enduring example of great thinking. But by setting them in context – and looking at the influences that shaped their authors, as well as the responses they provoked – Macat encourages readers to look at these classics and game-changers with fresh eyes. Readers learn to think, engage and challenge their ideas, rather than simply accepting them.

'Macat offers an amazing first-of-its-kind tool for interdisciplinary learning and research. Its focus on works that transformed their disciplines and its rigorous approach, drawing on the world's leading experts and educational institutions, opens up a world-class education to anyone.'

**Andreas Schleicher**
Director for Education and Skills, Organisation for Economic Co-operation and Development

'Macat is taking on some of the major challenges in university education … They have drawn together a strong team of active academics who are producing teaching materials that are novel in the breadth of their approach.'

**Prof Lord Broers,**
former Vice-Chancellor of the University of Cambridge

'The Macat vision is exceptionally exciting. It focuses upon new modes of learning which analyse and explain seminal texts which have profoundly influenced world thinking and so social and economic development. It promotes the kind of critical thinking which is essential for any society and economy. This is the learning of the future.'

**Rt Hon Charles Clarke, former UK Secretary of State for Education**

'The Macat analyses provide immediate access to the critical conversation surrounding the books that have shaped their respective discipline, which will make them an invaluable resource to all of those, students and teachers, working in the field.'

**Professor William Tronzo, University of California at San Diego**

# WAYS IN TO THE TEXT

## KEY POINTS

- Thomas Paine (1737–1809) was a radical English political philosopher and social reformer who supported both the American* and French Revolutions.*

- *Rights of Man* argues that the people have the right to revolt when the government fails to defend their rights.

- The text has inspired social movements around the world and has contributed much to the development of liberal democracy.*

### Who Was Thomas Paine?

Thomas Paine was born in Thetford, in Norfolk, England in 1737. The son of a Quaker* father and an Anglican* mother, he had a humble, religious upbringing and very little formal education. In 1774, at the age of 37, Paine met the great American statesman Benjamin Franklin* in London. Franklin recommended that Paine emigrate to the United States, and provided him with a letter of invitation to do so. After his arrival in Pennsylvania, Paine became an influential journalist and co-editor at the *Pennsylvania Magazine*. His writings were inspired by the revolutionary spirit of the American colonists in the Thirteen Colonies,* who struggled for independence from British rule. Paine was a radical and believed America had the right to revolt because the King of England imposed taxes on

Americans but did not allow them representation in the Parliament of Westminster. In 1776, he wrote his pamphlet *Common Sense*, urging the colonies to separate from Britain and form a republic.*

In 1787, Paine returned to England. Two years later, he took part in the French Revolution. Then, between 1791 and 1792, he wrote *Rights of Man* in two parts. Using everyday, direct language, he used the work to defend the right of people without financial privilege, social position, or institutional authority to revolt against the French aristocracy.* This second major work, which built on his radical vision in *Common Sense*, cemented Paine's historical legacy.

## What Does *Rights of Man* Say?

The first part of *Rights of Man* is a direct response to the Irish statesman and political thinker Edmund Burke,* who in 1790 published *Reflections on the Revolution in France*. In it, Burke posed the question: Was the French Revolution good for France and would such a revolution be good for England? He responded emphatically that the French Revolution was an atrocity that England should prevent at all cost. He argued that popular revolt was not permissible because the people were obliged to respect the norms and laws established by English rulers over many centuries.

Paine firmly disagreed. In part one of *Rights of Man* he argues that the French Revolution, like the American Revolution, was justified because the French monarchy* was corrupt, abusive, and responsible for the inequalities of society, notably unemployment and poverty. Paine's argument is worth considering if for no other reason than the fact that he witnessed the American Revolution and participated in the French Revolution. This gave him a privileged view of the changes those conflicts brought about—and how they empowered the common people of both nations.

In part two of his book Paine puts forward the idea that a republican form of government* with an elected head and based on representative democracy* is the best system for all nations, regardless of size. Paine believed that a republic should aspire to encourage the individuality of its citizens—even as they worked to pursue the common good—and that all people possessed certain natural rights* simply because they were human.

Part two also contains some of Paine's most original political theory. Here he outlines the difference between what he calls "old systems of government"—where entrenched rulers inherited their right to govern over the people, as they did in England—and "new systems" that gave the people a direct voice in their affairs. He mounts a passionate defense of representation as the best way to attain the goals of government.

He also outlines a series of reforms and social programs that English rulers should enact to improve the lives of the unemployed and poor. Paine's vision was conditioned by his own ordinary personal background and was part of his lifelong commitment to morality and social justice. It took many parts of the world (including Paine's adopted homeland of the United States) some time to catch up with aspects of his thinking and vision. For example, in *Rights of Man* Paine argues for the end of slavery; this was more than 70 years before US President Abraham Lincoln* freed American slaves in 1863.

### Why Does *Rights of Man* Matter?

Thomas Paine argued against the system of aristocrats ruling merely because of their social position and their children continuing to rule merely because of the circumstances of their birth (hereditary succession).* He claimed that popular political revolution was acceptable against government when it failed to safeguard the natural rights of the people. For this reason he supported both the American and the French Revolutions. Paine's radical vision inspired the reform movement* in nineteenth-century England, the anti-slavery movement in nineteenth-century America, and twentieth-century struggles in Africa and Asia against European colonial* powers. Paine's writings have also influenced the development of liberal democracy,* where elected representatives operate under a constitution that emphasizes the protection of individual rights and equality. His work has also had an impact on the following areas:

- Republican government—where the head of government is not selected by hereditary methods, but by other mechanisms, most often elections.
- Popular sovereignty*—where the authority of government is created and sustained by the consent of the people.
- Human rights—rights that are believed to belong to every person.
- The welfare state*—where the state agrees to protect the well-being of its citizens, often in relation to health.
- Social justice—justice in terms of the distribution of opportunities in a society.

While it's arguable that all these changes could have happened eventually, a direct line connects *Rights of Man* to the most sweeping political and social reforms in modern history. Paine tried to open up a debate about the injustices of aristocratic rule, how governments could be accepted as legitimate, and the duties of those who governed. In *Rights of Man* Paine also questioned and tackled social inequality head on and championed a strong system of taxation and redistribution of wealth. In the face of an entrenched British monarchy, Paine's work was clearly extremely radical.

Yet without raising a militia or firing a single gunshot, Paine helped bring about worldwide reforms and revolutions, while starting debates that are still happening today. *Rights of Man* was not a purely academic text. It was a radical roadmap—simple, sharp, and designed to reach common people—that showed how to create real and lasting reforms to benefit the poor and powerless. Paine understood, as perhaps no other writer of his time did, that he needed to reach an audience that was beyond the realm of statesmen alone. Through his writings, commoners were made aware of both the injustice of the aristocratic order and a way to eradicate it.

Because Paine both witnessed and played a role in the French Revolution, he knew how much power the people could potentially have. He saw what happened in France in 1789 not as a one-off event, but as a template that could apply anywhere where leaders had inherited power and had denied people their individual rights.

It can be argued that without *Rights of Man*, many ordinary people in many different places would have lived very different lives. When Paine raised his voice he gave people real hope. But he gave them more than that. He encouraged people to rise up and change the course of nations towards liberty, equality, and the welfare of everybody, not just a privileged few.

# SECTION 1
## INFLUENCES

# MODULE 1
# THE AUTHOR AND THE
# HISTORICAL CONTEXT

## KEY POINTS

- *Rights of Man* influenced the reform movement* in nineteenth-century England and the anti-slavery movement in America of the same period. In the twentieth century it also shaped anti-colonial struggles* against European powers in Africa and Asia. It has played a major role in the development of liberal democracy.*

- Paine's modest upbringing—where he suffered adversity and hardship—affected his lifelong commitment to morality and social justice.

- Paine's participation in the French Revolution* and his views on the American Revolution* shaped his radical political, economic, and social vision.

### Why Read This Text?

First published in 1791, Thomas Paine's *Rights of Man* has played an important role in the making of the modern world. In the nineteenth century it influenced the reform movement in England and the anti-slavery movement in America. In the twentieth century it had an effect on anti-colonial struggles in Africa and Asia against European powers. It has also proved an inspiration for many progressive* politicians, activists, and religious freethinkers.*

Many of the ideas Paine puts forward in the text were already circulating at the time of its writing. But *Rights of Man* inventively and persuasively stated principles that later became central to the ideas of liberal democracy, where elected representatives of the

> ❝ Contributing fundamentally to the American Revolution, the French Revolution, and the struggles of British workers in the Industrial Revolution, Thomas Paine was one of the most remarkable political writers of the modern world and the greatest radical of a radical age.[1] ❞
>
> Harvey Kaye,* *Thomas Paine and the Promise of America*

people govern, rather than those who govern simply because of their birth, like kings. Paine's ideas also had a major influence on many other areas:

- Universal rights*—rights to which all people are entitled simply because they are human.
- Republican government*—a system where the head of government is not there because of their birth, but by another mechanism, most often election.
- Popular sovereignty*—the idea that the authority of the government comes from the consent of the people.
- The welfare state*—where the state plays a central role in the well-being of its citizens.

Paine deliberately talked about his radical ideas in a way that would reach a wide popular audience. Through his writings, thousands of common men and women recognized injustice in an aristocratic* order where the nobles held all the power, and started to see ways to dismantle it.

Paine's ideas have led to an improvement in social conditions spanning centuries. But the author is as important as his ideas. Thomas Paine's whole life is still a fine example of passionate commitment to beliefs.

## Author's Life

Thomas Paine was born in 1737 in Thetford, a town in the rural English county of Norfolk. The son of a poor Quaker* father and an Anglican* mother, Paine was educated in a grammar school until the age of 13. He left to work with his father as a stay-maker,* someone who made corsets. Then, as a teenager, he left home for a time to become a sailor, but was working back on land in Britain by 1759.

Despite the political and theoretical content in *Rights of Man*, Paine never trained as a political philosopher. The individuals he met throughout his life and the events he witnessed influenced him more than the books he read. As the son of poor parents, he could see early in his life how the working class constantly fought for survival in a society that appeared happy to endorse privilege and inequality. This shaped his views on the role of the government and eventually led him to propose strong welfare policies to help the poor and those in society's lower ranks.

Paine's first wife and child died in childbirth, while a second marriage ended after the collapse of his store selling textiles and clothes in the southern English town of Lewes. Paine moved to London where a mutual friend introduced him to American publisher, politician, and activist Benjamin Franklin.* On Franklin's advice, and armed with a letter of recommendation from him, Paine left England for the New World* in October 1774.

Up to this point Paine had barely engaged in politics. But after arriving in Pennsylvania he became an influential journalist and started addressing political issues. His 1775 pamphlet *Common Sense* argued that America was the only place where freedom could blossom, especially when compared to Europe's decadent political regimes. Paine's views influenced the latter part of the American Revolution,* which took place between 1765 and 1783.

Right up until his death at a farm in New Rochelle, New York in 1809, Paine was a fearless and outspoken campaigner for his radical principles. He never accepted money for his work and lived in difficult financial conditions throughout his life. The British government persecuted him. He was almost killed during the violent period of the French Revolution* known as the Terror.* He was generally despised by the privileged establishment he attacked. And he was never recognized as one of America's Founding Fathers,* despite his major contribution to the beginnings of the United States. Yet Thomas Paine never gave up on his beliefs.

Paine's numerous accomplishments included detailed analyses of the French and American Revolutions, in which he played a part. He expanded political debate, encouraging those without financial privilege, social rank, or institutional authority to take part.

Finally, he established theoretical and political links between the struggles for freedom in America and France. Paine not only did this in his writings (especially *Rights of Man*) but also through his actions. One of Paine's biographers has even claimed that he "truly was, and remains, the greatest radical of this revolutionary age."[2]

## Author's Background
*Rights of Man* incorporates Paine's first-hand account of the French Revolution. It offers a passionate defense of its purpose and outcome that counters the criticisms of Irish statesman, political thinker, and orator Edmund Burke,* whose *Reflections on the Revolution in France* was a scathing attack on what had happened in France and a warning of dire consequences should the same thing happen in England.

*Rights of Man* was not an original title for a book. The expression was already in use in English philosopher John Locke's* *Second Treatise Concerning Civil Government* and in the important French Revolution document, the Declaration of the Rights of Man and of the Citizen.*

But Paine's choice of wording was deliberate. It confirmed his commitment to the idea that men and women have rights simply because they are born as human beings. He also believed that a general belief in these universal natural rights* sparked the French Revolution and the setting up of a republican government.

Paine wrote *Rights of Man* in two parts. He finished the first part on January 29, 1791 but it didn't become available until March 13 because the publisher feared consequences from the English government. Paine's views were highly controversial and he fled to France in 1791 after being persecuted by people who were loyal to the king. Having arrived in France he joined the Revolution and was even elected to the new assembly called the National Convention.* The English government tried to discredit Paine by questioning his loyalty and honor. In response Paine wrote a second part of *Rights of Man*, called "Combining Principle and Practice." Here he outlined reforms and social programs to improve the lives of England's poor.

The American and the French Revolutions shaped Paine's views on citizens' rights, as well as the role of government and its relationship to society. Though Paine had endured adversity and hardship in voicing these views, his experiences shaped his strong commitment to social justice.

## NOTES

1   Harvey J. Kaye, *Thomas Paine and the Promise of America* (New York: Hill and Wang, 2005), 4.

2   Harvey J. Kaye, *Thomas Paine: Firebrand of the Revolution* (New York: Oxford University Press, 2000), 144.

# MODULE 2
# ACADEMIC CONTEXT

## KEY POINTS

- When Thomas Paine wrote *Rights of Man* in 1791 the great political debate was about deciding which was the better form of government: a republic* or a monarchy.*

- The Enlightenment* movement of the time looked to science and reason for answers. This "logical" approach provided a backdrop for criticisms of the aristocracy* being born to rule and fostered ideas of republicanism,* where ordinary people would have more say about how they were governed.

- Paine's ideas led him to speak out loudly against aristocratic rule and hereditary succession.*

### The Work in Its Context

Thomas Paine wrote *Rights of Man* as the Western world was experiencing deep social and political transformations. The American Revolution* had just taken place, with the United States declaring independence in 1776. The French Revolution* had also overthrown the *ancien régime**—the old political and social system—in 1789 and the country had made a bold statement about individual rights that same year with their Declaration of the Rights of Man and of the Citizen.* Many conservatives in England, such as Irish statesman and political thinker Edmund Burke,* feared this situation could happen in England and that the monarchy could be in danger.

It was the Age of Enlightenment, characterized by a belief that people should look to science and reason for answers. A new wave of thinkers challenged ideas that had developed through tradition, superstition, or faith. They championed the pursuit of knowledge

> 66 The whole 'project' of *Rights of Man*, then, was in the first instance an attempt to marry the ideas of the American and French Revolutions, and in the second an attempt to disseminate these ideas in Britain. For Paine, these objectives were essentially three facets of the same symbol. For Burke, they were radically incompatible.[1] 99
>
> Christopher Hitchens,* *Thomas Paine's* Rights of Man: A Biography

through scientific methods and believed that human beings could take responsibility for their own lives. In the world of politics, these ideas bolstered the theory that government should be empowered only by the will of the people who could limit what it could do and influence the way it behaved. There could be no place for an imposed and often authoritarian regime.

The concepts Paine develops in *Rights of Man* proved central to political debate when he wrote it. These included the existence of universal natural rights,* the illegitimacy of hereditary aristocratic governments, and the need to limit the state's power over individuals. Paine saw the common men of his day as the inheritors and guardians of a new form of political rule.

### Overview of the Field

On one side of the political spectrum conservatives such as Burke criticized the French Revolution. They looked to prove that the idea of aristocratic government was a just one and so the status quo should be preserved. Burke argued that England had already weathered a popular revolution in 1688—the Glorious Revolution*— that achieved a stable balance between the monarchy and the people. He was concerned at what a further revolt might bring, arguing that it was both illogical and irreligious, given that the monarchy had been put in place by God.

On the other side, voices of British radicals defended the people's right to resist tyranny. They argued for rule by the consent of the governed. Paine entered a political arena marked by deep disagreement and campaigned for a revolutionary agenda. He argued for an end to slavery, for human freedom and natural rights, and for a legitimate government that supported the poor and underprivileged. In contrast to Burke, Paine maintained that the people had a right to instigate political revolution. In *Rights of Man*, he launches an attack on the aristocracy in common language meant to connect with a largely uneducated audience. He exposes the contradictions of rule by monarchy and highlights the abuses that had come about because of it. He did so to inspire the English working class to unite and do away with a broken, oppressive system.

### Academic Influences

In *Rights of Man*, Thomas Paine explicitly affirms that he "neither read books, nor studied other people's opinion. I thought for myself."[2] As he was well known for his independent views, his influences are hard to identify. Paine left formal education when he was just 13, but *Rights of Man* in particular shows that he was likely to have been deeply inspired by the English philosopher John Locke.* He shared Locke's firm belief in government by consent, the existence of natural rights and liberties, and the people's right to resistance and revolution.

It is also likely that Paine was influenced by French Enlightenment thinkers such as Montesquieu* and Voltaire,* as well as Genevan philosopher Jean-Jacques Rousseau.* Though Paine believed republicanism was the best form of government, he cannot be seen as a traditional republican. For Paine, a republic should still look to encourage the individuality of its citizens—even though those citizens should work together for the common good.

Some scholars have argued that American revolutionary and statesman Benjamin Franklin* was Paine's greatest mentor.[3] Like

Paine, Franklin championed liberty, democracy, and equality wherever natural rights were denied. What is clear is that both men had an enormous influence in both America and Europe.

## NOTES

1    Christopher Hitchens, *Thomas Paine's* Rights of Man: *A Biography* (New York: Grove Press, 2006), 16.

2    Thomas Paine, *Rights of Man* (London: Collector's Library, 2004), 261.

3    See, for example, Alfred Owen Aldridge, *Thomas Paine's American Ideology* (Newark: University of Delaware Press, 1984), 154.

# MODULE 3
# THE PROBLEM

## KEY POINTS

- In *Rights of Man* Thomas Paine defends the idea that all men had certain rights simply because they were human beings. He also addresses what constitutes a legitimate government.

- Paine wrote *Rights of Man* as a response to Edmund Burke's* Reflections on the Revolution in France, which argued that the English monarchy* should be preserved and protected in the face of radicalism.

- Paine denounces Burke's claim that a revolution is illegitimate, arguing that the people should not comply with unjust rules made by previous generations.

### Core Question

Thomas Paine's *Rights of Man* is not organized as a structured academic work. Rather, the book is a mix of accounts of events (or narratives), arguments based on Paine's principles, and statements designed to appeal to the reader. Its main goal is to defend the inalienable* rights of man, but it also tackles the issue of what a legitimate government is and how it can be set up. It is clear to Paine that these two questions cannot be looked at separately.

Paine argues that since human beings are entitled to natural rights,* a legitimate government can only be founded on "the common interest of society and the common rights of man."[2] So he provides a twofold view, which first develops his theory of legitimate government. He intertwines this with a historical account of the just nature of France's revolution* and its newly instituted government.

❝ Paine's reputation rests chiefly upon his great political works, *Common Sense*, which did much to spark the American Revolution, and *Rights of Man*, whose popularity was even greater and set off a much more extensive political debate. Paradoxically, however, Paine's very success also underlies his relative neglect as a thinker today. He was not a trained political philosopher, but a common man with an uncommonly sharp mind who was profoundly angered by the oppression and arrogance of Britain's upper classes as well as by hereditary rule generally.[1] ❞

Gregory Claeys, *Thomas Paine: Social and Political Thought*

As he considers his first set of questions, Paine also examines the defects of monarchical and aristocratic* forms of rule, even as he provides a practical agenda for reforming England. If his subject is hardly novel in politics, it is clearly one of its most important themes, because so many influential thinkers have addressed the topic, including the respected philosophers Jean-Jacques Rousseau,* John Locke,* and Thomas Hobbes.*

From a socio-political perspective, issues of natural rights and legitimate government are hugely relevant. Once rights are believed to be natural for all human beings—and not just a concept—then these rights do not rely upon the approval of a government: rather, they work to regulate a government's actions. And if society does not depend on the government in order to regulate itself, then government becomes a matter of choice and not necessity. Therefore, this allows for a deeper intervention of citizens in public affairs. This was a profound conclusion for Paine's time.

Paine approaches these issues in a broad enough fashion to reach beyond the particular case of the French Revolution, even though he offers an insightful historical account of it. Indeed, *Rights of Man* provides a well-articulated, principled theory of how an acceptance of natural rights leads to legitimate government. It should be noted that Paine's theory does not stand apart from the mainstream in terms of how he understood rights and the sources of governmental legitimacy. But Paine took his ideas straight to the people thanks to his accessible style. As a result, his timely analysis and passionate commitment to his ideals managed to connect with ordinary people.

## The Participants

Paine wrote *Rights of Man* as a direct, explicit response to statesman and political thinker Edmund Burke's *Reflections on the Revolution in France*, a 1790 pamphlet and masterpiece of modern conservatism.* Burke opposed the French Revolution and argued that the traditional English aristocracy should be protected against radicalism. His conclusion prompted a wave of responses by progressive* English writers.

The theoretical hostility between these two thinkers was so influential and so apparent that it became widely known as the "Burke–Paine debate." It was the first debate to establish that "the battleground of politics would long be dominated by the siege of aristocratic 'tradition' by plebeian* 'democracy.'"[3]

The disagreement between Paine and Burke also represented a larger ideological battle in Britain. This was an internal development that happened as revolutions swept away colonial* rule in the New World* and the old order in France. Every serious intellectual or politician chose a side. Either they stood in favor of reason, justice, and universal rights* advanced by the American* and the French Revolutions, or they campaigned for continuing the *ancien régime**—the rule of the old guard.

## The Contemporary Debate

While Burke attacked the French Revolution and its principles, Paine wanted to demonstrate that the deep transformations in politics and society that were taking place in France were legitimate. He denounced Burke's claim that a revolution was an illegitimate action because a society was obliged to comply with agreements that had been established with governments in previous generations. Burke argued that an unbreakable social contract must exist in all society, made between all generations under God. And given that the king was an extension of God on earth, then the king should govern and be respected by his subjects.

While Burke's *Reflections* provoked more than 50 critical responses,[4] *Rights of Man* received more than 500 reactions, from broadsheet newspapers to extensive essays.[5] The pamphlet played a major role in spreading the word of the British radical movement* of the 1790s. It inspired people outside the aristocracy to develop a new self-understanding and sustained a remarkable idea—that they too had a right to freedom, happiness, and political participation. This gave birth to what became known as the "Painite* movement," from mid-1792 to the spring of 1793.[6] The vision Thomas Paine put forward still resonates today.

## NOTES

1  Gregory Claeys, *Thomas Paine: Social and Political Thought* (Boston: Unwin Hyman, 1989), 2.

2  Thomas Paine, *Rights of Man* (London: Collector's Library, 2004), 65.

3  Claeys, *Thomas Paine*, 6.

4  Claeys, *Thomas Paine*, 67.

5  Claeys, *Thomas Paine*, 3.

6  Claeys, *Thomas Paine*, 114.

# MODULE 4
# THE AUTHOR'S CONTRIBUTION

## KEY POINTS

- Paine argued that the people have a right to revolt against illegitimate government.

- He challenged aristocratic* rule and championed republicanism.*

- Paine's vision was formed out of the contemporary political debates and social struggles. Although he never received formal training in political philosophy, he may well have been influenced by John Locke's* beliefs in natural rights* and the consent of the governed as a basis for government.

### Author's Aims

In *Rights of Man*, Thomas Paine makes his immediate aim clear in the opening paragraphs—and even on the title page of his work. He is seeking to challenge Irish statesman and political thinker Edmund Burke's* conservative pamphlet *Reflections on the Revolution in France*. Paine was not the only writer to take up the task of responding to Burke's pamphlet. He was not even the first to do so, but he ranks among the most successful.

For Paine, France provided an example that England should follow. By convincing the British public of the French Revolution's* legitimacy he hoped to spread revolutionary seeds throughout his homeland. Moreover, he said he was in favor of including the common people of England in the sphere of public political debate, one that had habitually excluded them for centuries.

> **❝** I know not whether any Man in the World has had more influence on its inhabitants or affairs for the last thirty years than Tom Paine ... Call it then the Age of Paine.[1] **❞**
>
> John Adams, President of the United States of America, 1797–1801, cited in Thomas Paine, *Common Sense*

Paine sought to ignite an open dialogue about universal natural rights,* how governments gained legitimacy, and the duties of those who governed. In *Rights of Man,* Paine questions the basis of aristocratic rule and social inequality. But beyond this, he also plants the seeds of historical change in England's political and social spheres. By laying the foundations of a real social struggle, Paine paved the way for popular political movements that would take England in the same revolutionary direction as America and France. But Paine did not just have theories: in his text he translated his aims into a coherent plan.

### Approach

The first part of the book was published just a few months after Burke's *Reflections on the Revolution in France* and carefully responds to every counter-revolutionary argument it made.

The second part advocates the reasoning behind and the potential of the republican system of government.* In addition, it offers a pointed critique of social injustice, something Paine believed could be defeated by the implementation of a strong system of taxation and wealth redistribution. Paine outlines each of his proposals clearly, presenting an impressive number of facts to support his more theoretical claims. Ever a frank and direct writer, Paine never conceals his intentions in the pamphlet.

Paine successfully transmits his ideas in common language and with great passion. These ideas were not in any way limited to one nation or restricted by a sense of nationalism* or patriotic feeling. He considered himself a "citizen of the world," a defender of justice everywhere. As he put it: "Independence is my happiness, and I view things as they are, without regard to place or person; my country is the world, and my religion is to do good."[2] This quotation sums up the vision that guided Paine in his lifelong struggle against aristocratic privilege and abuse.

## Contribution in Context

Although *Rights of Man* crystallizes and borrows from intellectual debates and social struggles of the time, it is hard to pinpoint just how much of it reflects ideas he developed from elsewhere. Thomas Paine never explicitly acknowledged his sources. He repeatedly argued that he would rather think for himself. Yet some analyses of Paine's views suggest that English philosopher John Locke was a major influence in developing his arguments. In particular, Locke's notions of government by consent of the people, basic freedoms and rights independent of social position, and the ultimate right of the people to revolt, can all be seen in Paine's arguments.[3]

Other important influences on Paine's thought include the writings of late eighteenth-century British law experts who dealt with issues of natural rights, and natural law.[4]

Paine had two main motivations to write *Rights of Man*. First, he believed it was both necessary and important to defend the French Revolution from severe English criticism. Second, Paine wanted to replace existing aristocratic institutions with new liberal ones that would give common people a voice.

But there was also a much bigger goal. Paine hoped to encourage the English lower classes to support revolution abroad and start one at home. He saw this as vital in order to make the huge changes he believed in. Paine wanted to see an end to slavery, pensions for older people, nationalization* of land and new laws regulating marriage and divorce. But his vision did not stop there. Paine also championed a family wage, maternity benefits, free education, prison reform, and full employment. He was also one of the first thinkers to propose international arbitration,\* while fearlessly opposing British colonialism\* in India and Africa. In these extraordinary aims, Paine was far ahead of his time and the issues he raised still form an important part of the agenda in both political and social debate over 200 years later.

## NOTES

1   Cited in Thomas Paine, *Common Sense*, ed. Isaac Kramnick (London: Penguin, 1976), 55.

2   Gregory Claeys, *Thomas Paine: Social and Political Thought* (Boston: Unwin Hyman, 1989), 105.

3   Jack Fruchtman, *The Political Philosophy of Thomas Paine* (Baltimore, MD: Johns Hopkins University Press, 2009), 5.

4   Claeys, *Thomas Paine,* 5.

# SECTION 2
# IDEAS

# MODULE 5
# MAIN IDEAS

## KEY POINTS

- The key themes of *Rights of Man* are: natural rights,\* the constitution,\* popular sovereignty,\* universal suffrage,\* and social justice.

- Paine's main argument is that hereditary succession\* and rule (as in a monarchy,\* for example) are illegitimate—he believes representative democracy\* is the best form of government for all nations.

- Paine presents these themes in a two-part work. The first is a challenge to Edmund Burke's\* *Reflections on the Revolution in France*. The second exposes the contradictions and abuses of the aristocracy\* and argues for a republican form of government.\*

### Key Themes

Thomas Paine's *Rights of Man* is divided into two parts, with the second written a year after the first.

The first part of the book challenges every argument put forward by statesman and political thinker Edmund Burke. In his essay *Reflections on the Revolution in France* Burke denounces the French Revolution\* as a danger to England's stability. Paine argues that those who fought for the French Revolution had done so believing in the natural rights of man. The preamble section of the United States Declaration of Independence\* (1776) reflects this concept. It states: "We hold these truths to be self-evident, that all men are created equal; they are endowed by their Creator with certain inalienable rights;\* that among these are life, liberty, and the pursuit of happiness."[2] Paine also evaluates the French Constitution and offers particular

> 66 Whatever is my right as a man is also the right of another; and it becomes my duty to guarantee as well as to possess.[1] 99
>
> Thomas Paine, *Rights of Man*

observations on one of the new declarations adopted in France after the revolution, namely the Declaration of the Rights of Man and of the Citizen.*

The second part of *Rights of Man* includes Paine's most original ideas about political theory. Here, he reinforces principles outlined in the first part of the work, while offering a practical agenda for reform. Paine distinguishes between government and society, stating that the latter only needs the former for the very few activities it cannot handle itself. Another important issue he addresses is the difference between what he calls "old systems of government" (hereditary) and "new systems" (representative). Paine mounts a passionate defense of representation as the best way to achieve the goals of government. He sees government and its constitution as two distinct, but connected, categories. Targeting the British government, Paine highlights its defects and outlines a detailed program of reforms, including progressive taxation* based on how much money an individual has and the redistribution of wealth.

Paine wrote the two parts of *Rights of Man* separately and with different purposes, so each has a distinct logic and argument. The first part claims Edmund Burke's argument in *Reflections on the Revolution in France* as misleading. Paine believes the French people have the right to overthrow an illegitimate government. The second part distinguishes between the political system of a constitution together with representative government, and the British government's foundation of inherited rule. Paine doesn't always order the themes logically and constantly repeats his arguments. But his plain and repetitive writing was part of a deliberate strategy to reach a broader public that did not have formal education.

The themes of natural rights, constitution, popular sovereignty, and universal suffrage* (or the right for each man to vote) unfold in a coherent way and form both a compelling attack on hereditary government and a persuasive defense of representative democracy.

### Exploring the Ideas

Paine's text is sweeping in its scope. He tackles the right of current generations to reassess and reestablish past agreements. He examines the French Revolution and how the emerging government differed from the British government of the day. He also distinguishes between society and government and the differences between the republican and aristocratic systems. He defines "constitution" and "popular sovereignty," argues for universal suffrage, and outlines the public measures needed to fight poverty and promote social equality.

This list might seem overly broad and hard to accommodate inside a single framework. But a careful analysis shows that these themes are better understood as interconnected parts of a theory of democratic republicanism.* The issues Paine tackles, however, all point to two key themes—a man's rights that cannot be taken away, and the need to destroy the privilege, corruption, and injustice that has been encouraged by governments based on the inheritance of rights.

It is difficult to say which key theme is most significant, but Paine unites these diverse ideas into a logical and cohesive whole. Yet the notion of universal individual rights is the most notable of them, as it effectively authorizes three key things: popular sovereignty, the right to revolt, and the claim to a legitimate and just government.

Two particular aspects of Paine's document demand attention for readers to gain a full understanding of his work. The first is historical, and concerns the French Revolution. Paine developed many arguments in *Rights of Man* out of his previous writings, particularly

1776's *Common Sense*. But the French Revolution and the debates it ignited throughout Europe gave him a chance to convert loose ideas into mature reasons based on natural rights. Central to this were representative government and popular sovereignty.

The second dimension is more theoretical. Paine's ideas sat within three different broader debates, as suggested by history professor Gregory Claeys.*[3] The first concerns the conventions, the constitutionalism,* and the republicanism that's needed if a political community is to craft rules for itself. The second involves the issues about the foundations and implications of natural rights and natural law.* The third considers the roles commerce, wealth, and social equality play in a political community.[4]

## Language and Expression

Paine understood that most people of his day lacked formal education, which excluded them from the important debates of the time. These included universal natural rights, the illegitimacy of the aristocracy and hereditary succession, as well as the need to limit the state's power over the individual. In *Rights of Man* he targets this audience—which had historically never taken part in the political process—as equals. Paine treats them as independent and rational beings who can reflect well and make sound decisions. This makes him a master of democratic prose.

Paine adopts straightforward, heartfelt language immediately accessible to people with little or no formal education. To do this, he often resorts to repetition. He restates many of his arguments throughout the book as a strategy to keep the reader with him. By making those issues connect to the lower classes of eighteenth-century England, Paine sharpened and animated the democratic ideals he was putting forward.

Religion also influenced Paine's thinking and he was happy to use religious language and scriptural images in his writings—to the point of sometimes sounding like a priest. Despite any personal religious feeling he may have had, Paine openly attacked organized religion, particularly in his book *The Age of Reason*.[5] He was in favor of the separation of church and state. He used religious language to encourage worldly reforms that would help people enjoy a heaven—of sorts—on Earth.

## NOTES

1   Cited in Alfred Owen Aldridge, *Thomas Paine's American Ideology* (Newark: University of Delaware Press, 1984), 128.

2   Preamble, Declaration of Independence, July 4, 1776, accessed March 13, 2015, http://www.archives.gov/exhibits/charters/declaration_transcript.html.

3   Gregory Claeys, *Thomas Paine: Social and Political Thought* (Boston: Unwin Hyman, 1989).

4   Claeys, *Thomas Paine*.

5   In *Age of Reason*, Thomas Paine challenged institutionalized religion, particularly Christianity, implicitly questioning the legitimacy of the Bible. The pamphlet was published in the United States, in three different parts, in 1794, 1795, and 1807.

# MODULE 6
# SECONDARY IDEAS

## KEY POINTS

- *Rights of Man* addresses these key secondary themes: social inequalities as a result of aristocratic rule* and hereditary succession;* commerce; and social justice and peace.
- Paine wanted to expose the abusive nature of aristocratic rule and show how it created social inequalities.
- His radical analysis of social inequalities provided context for the later development of economic redistribution and social welfare* policies.

### Other Ideas

Key secondary themes in Thomas Paine's *Rights of Man* include:

- the aristocracy and hereditary succession
- commerce
- social justice and peace

While these themes might appear not to have much to do with each other, they are in fact closely linked to the main issues Paine addresses. They provide his account with a firmer basis and articulate, in a very clear way, what Paine's core thesis actually meant in the real world.

Paine portrays the aristocratic system as one based on corruption and unjust privilege that denied the majority of the population its natural rights.* He also attacks the idea of hereditary succession based on whom a person was descended from, which he argued was deeply unjust. Paine believed that the people should revolt against this system

> ❝ He [Thomas Paine] sought to destroy oligarchy [rule by an elite few], but to supplant this by republican rule in the name of the common good by all citizens, not the narrow rule of a single class. The commercial prosperity which would follow the revolution, too, was to benefit all classes, its new wealth spreading like water across an arid landscape. It was expected not to increase economic inequality, but to curtail it.[1] ❞
>
> Gregory Claeys, *Thomas Paine: Social and Political Thought*

wherever it existed and replace it with a republican form of government.* This form of government should be based on individual rights, popular sovereignty* of the people, the consent of the governed, and constitutional* law. Paine was convinced this would eradicate centuries of injustice and work for the common good rather than that of the privileged few.

Following the same line of thought, Paine argues that commerce and taxes must benefit all society. In his view, progressive taxation* and economic redistribution helped to guarantee the general well-being of society. These twin reforms would address the growing problems of inequality, unemployment, and poverty.

### Exploring the Ideas

In *Rights of Man*, Paine develops important secondary ideas. First, he forcefully critiques the aristocracy and the idea of rule based on hereditary succession. Paine attacks the problems with Britain's government and class system on at least three different fronts. First, he argues that parliamentary representation is limited and unfairly distributed. It fails the social groups it seeks to represent, producing legislation that is not fit for purpose. Second, the taxation system exempts the aristocracy and overtaxes the poor. Finally, the monopolies

established by aristocratic groups curb commercial freedom—
something Paine believed had civilizing potential.

In outlining the situation in Britain, Paine suggests his home
country should follow the revolutionary examples of the United
States of America and France. But he also calls for international
military alliances, which he believes will permit each nation state to
reduce its war expenses. As a result, more public funding would remain
for social welfare. For Paine, the international expansion of
revolutionary values would strengthen cooperation and tolerance
among the nations, while furthering commercial exchange

His second and third criticisms connect: commerce would
strengthen civilization's values. Paine saw commerce as a system that
promoted peace as individuals cooperate to fulfil their mutual needs.
War between nations, then, and the taxation of domestic consumer
goods strained commercial development.

Paine's beliefs regarding commerce and minimal government
might suggest a libertarian* viewpoint, that government should be
reduced to the minimum necessary to protect the liberty of the state's
citizens. But he also outlines a welfare system that favors the poor. He
says that inequality and injustice were caused by the political, rather
than the economic system, and this could be changed through
progressive taxation and cuts on unnecessary expenditure. Paine stops
short of suggesting private property should be abolished, but
understands that property disputes should not cause unnecessary
problems in a world that operates on mutual benefit.

### Overlooked

Political theory scholarship has overlooked at least two aspects of
Thomas Paine's *Rights of Man*.

The first is Paine's theory of representation. Today, representative
democracy* is often considered a necessary evil. Though it allows
long-established democratic ideals to continue among massive

populations and territories, it is managed by a distinct political class—and they serve a social and economic elite. As much as this system both constricts and reduces democracy, it is still a form of democracy, even if it is compromised.

However, Paine saw representation as more democratic than direct democracy* itself. For him, representative democracy allows different sections of society to integrate through the exchange of practical knowledge and experience. As part of its primary purpose, he believes a parliament could provide a center for this type of exchange.

Paine developed his theory of representation in a practical rather than an abstract way. He claimed all individuals in a democracy are equal. As a result, their experiences should be properly represented in a model where government unites power and knowledge.

Finally, Paine saw representation as a benchmark of political modernity, alongside individual rights. But there has not been a specific and detailed assessment of Paine's idea. Existing literature simply discusses his commitment to representative democracy without paying attention to the innovative nature of his model.

The second neglected element of *Rights of Man* relates to Paine's understanding of cosmopolitanism.* The last 20 years have seen a resurgence of debates among political theorists as to what this means. Deriving from the Greek word *kosmopolites* ("citizen of the world"), the term "cosmopolitanism" describes socio-political views that share a core idea: all humans, regardless of nationality, should be considered citizens in a single community. Yet from this starting point theorists differ as to what cosmopolitanism really means in terms of institutions, rights, and obligations.

Paine himself lived a cosmopolitan life. A citizen of the world, he had no ties to anything other than his ideals of freedom and democracy. Although referred to as a "radical cosmopolitan," no one has tried to fathom the foundation and practical implications of the term as Paine understood it.

These two aspects of Paine's work are ripe for reconsideration and reinterpretation. A deeper appreciation of Paine's theory of representation could yield fresh perspectives in the current debate on the limits of representative democracy. At a time when all types of democrats* have attacked the representative model for its flaws, Paine's views could provide new, stronger foundations. Along the same lines, benefits might well be gained by re-examining the idea of cosmopolitanism, both from Paine's theory and from his practical calls for action. It would not only contribute to broadening the current debates on the theme, but also spark a reassessment of Paine's work as a whole. In either case, Paine's vision would benefit from the appraisal of fresh eyes.

## NOTES

1   Gregory Claeys, *Thomas Paine: Social and Political Thought* (Boston: Unwin Hyman, 1989), 59.

# MODULE 7
# ACHIEVEMENT

## KEY POINTS

- Paine's ideas about natural rights* and popular sovereignty* are important elements of modern political theory.

- Paine played an instrumental role in both the American* and French Revolutions.*

- His plain, passionate language proved the most important factor in making his views heard by huge numbers of people.

### Assessing the Argument

Thomas Paine's *Rights of Man* articulates ideas that were already current in British radical circles, including the right to resist tyranny and rule by the consent of the governed. Yet Paine formulated these notions in an innovative way that has endured into the twenty-first century. His depiction of both natural rights and popular sovereignty remains relevant to the study of modern political theory. This is for two particular reasons.

First, Paine articulated the concept of democratic revolution as a pathway to provoke social and political change. He argued that citizens have the right to revolt against an illegitimate government and create another one, founded on the commitment to ensure popular sovereignty and human natural rights. This radical, simple idea still applies today in a world where oppressive governments continue to dominate common citizens.

Second, Paine rejected the idea that only a few enlightened men could understand politics and participate in it. As a result, he

> ❝ God save great Thomas Paine,
> His *Rights of Man* explain to every soul.
> He makes the blind to see what dupes and slaves they be,
> and points out liberty from pole to pole ...[1] ❞
>
> Joseph Mather, "God Save Great Thomas Paine"

established a type of writing—"democratic prose"—to prove his point. Rather than address an exclusive group of educated readers, Paine tried to transform political language into an instrument that any person could use. Paine wrote in a plain style that resembled everyday speech and avoided references to classical thinkers. He brought the language of ordinary people into political debate, transforming it in the process. Paine's style and vision can certainly be seen reflected in US President Abraham Lincoln's* Gettysburg Address of 1863, where he referred to "government of the people, by the people, for the people."

Paine's writing was revolutionary not only because of its content, but also because of its form. He renounced an old elitist tradition and started a style that still lives today, enlarging the political sphere to embrace common people as active participants.

### Achievement in Context
When Paine published *Rights of Man* in 1791 it was widely distributed and read by all social classes. Estimates suggest that around 100,000 copies were sold in the first two years after publication.[2] This was a clear indication that his work had political influence. The authorities were worried about the ideas Paine was putting in people's heads. He was tried and convicted in England in his absence for seditious libel,* conduct that the authorities believed encouraged people to revolt against the established order.

Despite the British government's efforts to silence Paine and control circulation of his radical ideas, his incendiary words spread widely. Paine's works, particularly *Rights of Man*, sold very well indeed and were printed and reprinted in various languages. His writings served as a source of knowledge, guidance, and inspiration for many. And the historical account of the French Revolution he provides in *Rights of Man* remains a valuable source.

Thomas Paine ranks among the great Western political thinkers for three main reasons. First, he developed his writings in a thoughtful and visionary manner, discussing themes and issues that have continuously been relevant to debates on governance. Second, he introduced a new style of political writing, known as "democratic prose." This way of writing succeeded in appealing to the masses because of its simplicity, directness, and avoidance of academic jargon and references. Thirdly, Paine became a source of inspiration for many future progressive* movements and freethinkers.*

### Limitations

Paine's work was suppressed and censored to a degree that had not been seen in England for a long time. When the government realized how popular *Rights of Man* was among the working class, it went on the offensive. Paine felt his liberty and maybe his life were in danger, so he escaped to France in 1792. He was convicted in his absence of authoring seditious* publications that were stirring up potentially revolutionary feelings. He never set foot in England again. His conviction was followed by a campaign against his supporters, some of whom were arrested for publicly reading or reproducing the text.[3]

Though Paine was feted in France for some years, he was also accused of associating with the outlawed political faction, the Girondists,* and spent almost a year in prison, narrowly avoiding execution.

Despite these efforts to silence him, Paine continued to speak out against injustice. He dedicated his life to defending oppressed peoples everywhere. As a result, he helped to shape both the American and French Revolutions, and also reforms in England. Not only did he inspire popular revolt against the aristocratic* powers of the time, but he also outlined how a more rational and just society could be organized. Broadly speaking, Paine's views have been an inspiration for the idea of liberal democracy* everywhere. Through *Rights of Man*, Paine breathes life into the cliché that the pen is mightier than the sword.

## NOTES

1   Joseph Mather, "God Save Great Thomas Paine," (1791), cited in Christopher Hitchens, *Thomas Paine's* Rights of Man*: A Biography* (New York: Grove Press, 2006), 3–4.

2   See, for example, Mark Philp, *Paine* (Oxford: Oxford University Press, 1989).

3   A. J. Ayer, *Thomas Paine* (Chicago: University of Chicago Press, 1988), 119.

# MODULE 8
# PLACE IN THE AUTHOR'S WORK

## KEY POINTS

- Paine's body of work attacked aristocratic* rule and hereditary succession*—as seen in a monarchy,* for example—and argued in favor of republicanism.*

- *Rights of Man* complemented his earlier work, Common Sense, which argued that America had the right to revolt against and overthrow the abusive British monarchy.

- The author's writings confirmed him as a radical political philosopher and social reformer.

### Positioning

Although Thomas Paine certainly ranks as a mature thinker, *Rights of Man* should primarily be considered as the work of a deeply engaged political campaigner. Paine became an international revolutionary and political agitator after leaving England for the New World* in 1774 at the age of 37. In the American colonies, Paine found himself caught up in the struggle against British imperial rule. The context of the American Revolution* would exert a powerful affect on Paine and his work. The ideas he would develop in 1791 in *Rights of Man* exist in embryonic form in his earlier pamphlet *Common Sense*, which Paine wrote in Philadelphia, Pennsylvania in 1776—in the same year and place where the United States declared its independence from Britain.

Paine published *The Age of Reason: Being an Investigation of True and Fabulous Theology*, written in three parts between 1794 and 1807. Here he defended deism,* the belief in a supreme being who is a creator, but who does not intervene in the universe or interact with humankind. Written in the spirit cultivated by the Enlightenment* and the French

> 66 Thomas Paine's *Rights of Man* is both a trumpet
> of inspiration and a carefully wrought blueprint for
> a more rational and decent ordering of society, both
> domestically and on the international scene.[1] 99
>
> Christopher Hitchens,* *Thomas Paine's* Rights of Man: *A Biography*

Revolution,* Paine's *Reason* analyzed institutionalized religion. Although he made it clear that all individuals should have the freedom to believe as they chose, he argued that the Church was a human invention. As such, it terrorized and enslaved mankind while reaping power and profit. This very much fitted into his wider vision, which attacked what he understood to be corruption, privilege, and oppression.

## Integration

The French Revolution inspired *Rights of Man*, which contains a principled, grounded defense of the movement against its critics, particularly Irish philosopher and orator Edmund Burke.* It is certainly Paine's masterpiece, containing a fully formed body of political ideas developed during the years he spent in Europe and America.

Published in 1776, over a decade before *Rights of Man*, *Common Sense* put up a defense of the idea of American independence from Britain and the republican government* in the colonies. Here Paine demonstrated that the problems America faced had their roots in monarchical rule. He further argued that the colonists could only truly free themselves by breaking completely with Britain's compromised form of government.

Paine arrived at the *Rights of Man*'s key concepts via three avenues. He reflected on his experiences in revolutionary America, analyzed the French Revolution, and formulated a critical account of contemporary British society. The ideas advanced in *Common Sense* provided plenty of raw material for Paine's masterpiece. The same recognizable writing style also forms another key element to both works: accessible to the common reader and connected to the goals of emancipation.

Paine's work is defined by his commitment to the notion that human beings hold natural rights* that cannot be curtailed or undermined—neither by society, nor government. Indeed these rights, Paine argues, work to regulate a government's actions. He continually expands this core idea, vigorously developed in *Rights of Man*, to attack monarchical and aristocratic rule. As a natural result of this view, he defends the republican form of government and calls for new institutional mechanisms to combat social injustice and poverty.

These interconnected arguments lead some to place Paine's work in the liberal* tradition of thought. This was the idea, as popularized in the nineteenth century, that the individual is central in life and that politics should protect and enhance individual freedom. But it is hard to categorize him as such because he also advocated republican government. In fact, Paine's radical political program merged representative democracy,* popular sovereignty,* natural rights, limited government, and welfare state* measures. This would make him a democratic* liberal thinker with an egalitarian bent.

Yet through his writing, Paine aimed to include the ordinary reader and citizen in the political debates from which they were excluded and encourage demands for more political participation and criticism. For this reason, Paine might be better categorized as a radical democrat with some liberal principles and an interest in civic duty.

## Significance

Divided into two parts written between 1791 and 1792, *Rights of Man* is intellectually unified and coherent. It offers a fully developed critique of despotism,* the form of government where the ruler has absolute power. It also puts forward a clear program for republican democratic government. Through his life Paine remained loyal to the political ideas he so forcefully advocated in *Rights of Man*. Rather than revise them, he even took them a step further in his criticism of institutionalized religion, *The Age of Reason*. *Rights of Man* paved the way for Paine to attack religious authority and anticipated his theory that God ordered the world, but was revealed to humanity through reason.

*Rights of Man* was widely distributed and read among all social classes. Estimates suggest about 100,000 copies were sold in the first two years after publication,[2] demonstrating that Paine's work had real influence.

Despite the British government's efforts to silence him and control circulation of his radical notions, Paine's words spread far and wide. What he wrote sold very well and his works were printed and reprinted in a number of languages. Many different elements of society viewed Paine's political writings as a source of knowledge, guidance, and inspiration. Not only this, but *Rights of Man* also provides a valuable historical resource thanks to its impressive account of the French Revolution.

## NOTES

1   Christopher Hitchens, *Thomas Paine's* Rights of Man*: A Biography*. (New York: Grove Press, 2006), 11.

2   See, for example, Mark Philp, *Paine* (Oxford: Oxford University Press, 1989).

# SECTION 3
# IMPACT

# MODULE 9
# THE FIRST RESPONSES

## KEY POINTS

- When *Rights of Man* was first published people on both sides of the political spectrum criticized it.

- Conservatives were against the work because they wanted to keep the status quo. Some progressives* disliked it, because they were scared about their own position and influence if common people were given too much power.

- Thomas Paine did not respond to his critics.

### Criticism

Both progressives and conservatives* criticized Thomas Paine's *Rights of Man*. Among the former, two very distinct types of criticism emerged.

The first progressives to question Paine came from within the ranks of the reform movement* in Britain. They criticized his ideas as too radical. In fact, reformists did not expect *Rights of Man* to have the impact it did and feared the political consequences of a popular reformist movement. They were worried that Paine's views would lead to people demanding too much. The reform movement, for example, did not count universal suffrage* (the right of all men to have the vote) and natural rights* as part of its political agenda. The reformists were mainly industrialists from the wealthy middle classes and limited themselves to challenging two particular ideas: one, a despotic* monarchy,* where one person had supreme authority and often abused that position; and two, destructive oligarchy,* where governmental power is confined to a few people or families. Rights, they argued, were primarily civil,* legally granted by a society to all

> **❝** For Burke, liberal democracy is an achievement of Western civilization, refined and improved gradually over many generations ... For Paine, liberal democracy is the application of principles discovered in the Enlightenment. It's a break, a sharp break, from everything that preceded the Enlightenment, and the purpose of politics is to further apply those principles ... And there you have the foundation of conservatism on the one hand and progressivism on the other.[1] **❞**
>
> Yuval Levin*, quoted in Nat Brown, "Edmund Burke v. Thomas Paine"

individuals in it. This is different from natural rights, which—according to Paine—belong to all human beings by the mere virtue of their existence.

The reformists were also skeptical about how the French Revolution* had unfolded and feared its spread to England. They accused Paine of reckless enthusiasm as he failed to consider the disastrous practical implications of ideas that incited the poor to resist injustice with violence. These people had always seen themselves as at the forefront of social change. Paine's anti-elitist concept of politics placed the common people at the center of the revolutionary movement and this frightened many reformists.[2]

The more radical political left, however, believed Paine was too moderate. Thomas Spence,* a London printer arrested for selling the second part of *Rights of Man*, argued that Paine did not go far enough, restricting himself to attacking the monarchy and its privileges without confronting what Spence believed was the root of social inequality—private property.[3]

English political philosopher and journalist William Godwin* also looked beyond Paine and rejected talk of "rights" altogether.

Instead, he was in favor of a moral understanding of communal duties and rejected popular political activism. He also called for a "community of goods"* to replace private property, which would move into "a trust for common use."[4]

There were many conservatives, meanwhile, who took against Paine's ideas. People loyal to the monarchy made verbal threats and used legal harassment and physical violence against anyone identified as a Painite.* They spread propaganda aimed at the working class and published material that ridiculed or distorted Paine's arguments. They argued that rights did not spring from human creation at all, but were derived from common law and the privileges of living Englishmen. For them, Paine's ideas were attempting to subvert a natural and balanced social order where inequality was a natural part of the order of things. They also rejected the right of each generation to create its own ideas of government. They believed institutions that had been around for a long time had proved their worth because of their durability. They praised the British system of checks and balances and maintained that the old existing documents that had already given certain liberties to Englishmen—such as the Magna Carta* and the Bill of Rights*—were already effectively a real constitution.

Finally, they insisted Paine misunderstood how humans built a civil society to overcome the chaos of a natural society. They argued that Paine wanted to reinstate an absolute equality between men that had never existed in the first place.[5]

### Responses
Paine never answered the critics of *Rights of Man*—or, at least, he never addressed them directly. Paine enjoyed standing at the center of important debates, but he always had his firm political convictions. He never abandoned them to defend himself from criticism.

Because the British government persecuted Paine for publishing *Rights of Man*, he was forced to escape to France. This might have contributed to his unwillingness or inability to take on his various critics.

Instead, when he arrived in France, Paine immediately got involved with the French Revolution and started writing with the aim of influencing local revolutionary politics.

Paine was very clear in both his seminal works, *Common Sense* and *Rights of Man*. In both documents he established himself as a defender of universal human rights and social justice. Throughout his life, Paine wrote about his ideas. But he also acted on them. His work as an activist in the American* and French Revolutions inspired others to follow him. He wrote and lived as a man of the people, and the people embraced both him and his ideas.

### Conflict and Consensus

Paine had a consistent and coherent political philosophy. In writings that spanned the period from 1776 until his death in 1809 he did not modify the major parts of his argument. Paine remained faithful to his original aims that he stated in an 1806 letter to the Mayor of the City of Philadelphia: "to rescue man from tyranny and false systems and false principles of government and enable him to be free, and establish government for himself."[6]

It is, however, possible to spot smaller changes in Paine's views in his writings. One concerns the specifics in various forms of government. Paine defended a republican government* in its simplest form for many years, rejecting the idea of what was called a bicameral legislature* (a governmental system with two houses, chambers, or branches). But the effectiveness of this system in the American Congress after 1789, the renovation of the Constitution of Pennsylvania after 1790, and the disintegration of France's National Convention* in 1793 saw Paine change his mind and decide that a bicameral system could more effectively develop policy and laws after all.[7]

Paine also modified his views on revolution. In *Rights of Man* he argued in favor of revolution as the only mechanism capable of producing real political change. But after the problems that emerged after the French Revolution, his own experience of being jailed in France during the Terror,* and a successful transition of power in America with the 1800 elections, Paine's views softened. He came to believe that the right to vote, granted to all men over 28, could prove more effective than direct revolutionary action.

Paine modified these original views, but in areas that were clearly less central to his overall theories. And it was personal experience that drove his changes of heart rather than other people criticizing his ideas. Paine wasn't a man to bend to his detractors.

## NOTES

1 Cited in Nat Brown, "Edmund Burke v. Thomas Paine," *National Review*, December 3, 2013, accessed February 23, 2015, http://www.nationalreview.com/article/365296/edmund-burke-v-thomas-paine-nat-brown.

2 Gregory Claeys, *Thomas Paine: Social and Political Thought* (Boston: Unwin Hyman, 1989).

3 Claeys, *Thomas Paine*, 134.

4 Claeys, *Thomas Paine*, 134.

5 Claeys, *Thomas Paine*, 150.

6 Jack Fruchtman, *The Political Philosophy of Thomas Paine* (Baltimore: Johns Hopkins University Press, 2009), 151.

7 Fruchtman, *Political Philosophy*, 153.

# MODULE 10
# THE EVOLVING DEBATE

## KEY POINTS

- Paine's core themes of rights and democracy* are central to modern life.

- Thomas Paine contributed to the development of "freethinking,"* and has clearly influenced radicals and social reformers.

- Paine's arguments and practical proposals have inspired and driven the thinking of progressive* movements around the world.

### Uses and Problems

Thomas Paine's works, notably *Rights of Man*, were everywhere both during his lifetime and after his death. His ideas, which became known throughout many different parts of society, had more influence in practical politics than in political theory. Following the Battle of Waterloo* in 1815 and victory over the French, Britain came to the end of a long period of war. The country moved into a period of industrialization, known as the Industrial Revolution,* which saw a number of radical economic and social changes as working habits were completely revolutionized. Understanding that a new world meant new challenges, particularly for the working class, the reform movement* rapidly gathered pace in England, galvanized by a number of elements of Paine's ideology. Many of his followers, or "Painites",* came from a radicalized working class.[2]

Paine's name and views—particularly his ideas about liberty, the role of commerce, and employment for the poor—returned to the center stage of politics during the discussions that led to the

> 66 For Paine, one thing was in fact clear: he knew that human beings had a natural love of liberty. And he knew too that people considered freedom as personal property, property of which no person could deprive others without violating nature.[1] 99
>
> Jack Fruchtman, "'Common Sense' and its Meaning Today by Jack Fruchtman"

Representation of the People Act* in 1832.[3] His words also inspired the working-class Chartist* movement of the nineteenth century as it looked to make the British political system more democratic.

Paine's ideas lost some of their appeal in reformist and revolutionary circles in the mid-nineteenth century because they lacked an economic element. By this time radical debates had shifted towards the language of economic rather than political relations to discuss and clarify the roots of working-class oppression.

For socialists,* particularly those influenced by the nineteenth-century thinker Robert Owen,* a worker's right to fair pay was more important to the activist agenda than the less immediate question of natural rights.* For political economists following the philosopher and reformer Jeremy Bentham,* the natural rights theory caused problems. Benthamites suggested that nothing could derive from nature besides power, so "rights" were therefore society's creation and, as such, could only be evaluated for their usefulness.

In the late twentieth century, however, universal human rights and consent of the governed became prominent issues discussed both inside and outside academia. They continue to be important to theoretical discussion and rights struggles in the twenty-first century. In the ongoing debate a consensus has emerged that humans are entitled to certain universal guarantees.

## Schools of Thought

Many individuals and groups have used Paine's text since its 1792 publication. Paine himself is recognized as a pioneer of "freethinking"—a mode of writing and argument that contests established truths and speculates beyond traditions, faith, authority, and attitudes.

One of Paine's freethinking disciples of the nineteenth century, Robert G. Ingersoll,* stands out for the important role he played in American politics. He also took at least some inspiration from Paine's views on religion in advocating agnosticism, the belief that God's existence can be neither proved nor disproved. Moreover, the Jeffersonian democracy movement* that existed in America between the 1790s and the 1820s relied on Paine's ideas and distributed *Rights of Man* to people at their meetings.

Paine greatly influenced English radicals of the nineteenth century who argued for the Reform Bill* in England to be passed. In 1837, George Julian Harney* and other Chartist leaders launched the manifesto of the East London Democratic Association,* which aimed to elevate living conditions for the working class. They accomplished this "by disseminating the principles propagated by that great philosopher and redeemer of mankind, the Immortal Thomas Paine."[4]

When James Bronterre O'Brien,* an Irish Chartist leader and journalist, contested the untouchable status of private property, Paine's writings, particularly *Agrarian Justice*, provided him with the arguments he needed. Finally, William Cobbett,* an English pamphleteer and journalist, abandoned his loyalist* position and became one of Paine's greatest followers.

For much of the second half of the nineteenth century Paine was to all intents and purposes forgotten. But in the United States of America he was rediscovered towards the end of the century by the great radical American poet Walt Whitman.* He was then restored to prominence in the twentieth century by socialist and union activist Eugene V. Debs.* Meanwhile, in England, historian E. P. Thompson* revived interest in

Paine's works and his role in radical movements with his groundbreaking 1963 text, *The Making of the English Working Class*.

As Paine himself did, his followers focused their interest on practical measures to transform the world, bypassing theoretical solutions. *Rights of Man* served as a resource and inspiration for how to do this.

## In Current Scholarship

Thomas Paine's works, including *Rights of Man*, have provoked strong responses of all kinds. Some people celebrate Paine as a champion of democracy and human rights. Others revile him as an atheist. But his thinking clearly helped drive progressive movements on both sides of the Atlantic throughout the nineteenth century. His views inspired democrats,* socialists, labor activists, and religious freethinkers.

In America Paine's work inspired the anti-slavery movement; the radical American abolitionist John Brown* said he had read Paine, while Paine's analysis of American society also inspired feminist Frances Wright* and socialist union leader Eugene Debs.

While it is difficult to identify political theorists who are true "disciples" of Paine, a revival in scholarship on his life and works began in the 1980s. He is now recognized as a major thinker of his time, known as the Age of Democratic Revolution.*[5]

In America, scholars have focused on Paine's role in their Revolution and how his ideas spur a continuing debate on democracy and representation.[6] In Britain, meanwhile, scholars have looked at the two opposing views expressed in books by Paine and philosopher Edmund Burke.* They have also examined Paine's role in socio-political developments of 1790s Britain. Important works, such as historian E. P. Thompson's* *The Making of the English Working Class*, have also explored his impact.

It may be excessive to say that Paine has a group of followers committed to reviving his views for the twenty-first century. But his role in shaping the modern world is widely acknowledged—

particularly considering the general agreement about the fundamental importance of democracy, human rights, equality, and the consent of the governed.

## NOTES

1   Jack Fruchtman, "'Common Sense' and its Meaning Today by Jack Fruchtman," The Thomas Paine National Historical Association and the Thomas Paine Foundation, January 26, 2001, accessed February 23, 2015, http://thomaspaine.org/aboutpaine/common-sense-and-its-meaning-today-by-jack-fruchtman.html.

2   Gregory Claeys, *Thomas Paine: Social and Political Thought* (Boston: Unwin Hyman, 1989), 210.

3   Claeys, *Thomas Paine*, 212.

4   Thomas Paine, *The Thomas Paine Reader*, eds. Michael Foot and Isaac Kramnick (Harmondsworth: Penguin, 1987), 33.

5   R. B. Bernstein, "Rediscovering Thomas Paine," *New York Law School Law Review* 39 (1994): 878.

6   See, for example, Eric Foner, *Tom Paine and Revolutionary America* (London: Oxford University Press, 1976).

# MODULE 11
# IMPACT AND INFLUENCE TODAY

## KEY POINTS

- *Rights of Man* is a seminal text of political philosophy that inspired progressive* thinkers and social movements.
- US President Barack Obama* quoted Thomas Paine in his 2009 inauguration speech.
- The principles found in *Rights of Man* are currently being challenged by both neoliberals* and those who believe in participatory democracy.*

## Position

Cheryl Hudson,* a fellow at the Rothermere American Institute at Oxford University, summarized Thomas Paine's contemporary relevance as follows: "At the center of his thought was a trust in the people ... He encouraged the public's aspiration for a better, more democratic world ... Today, political leaders on both sides of the Atlantic pay lip service to concepts like political empowerment but Paine truly believed in the transformative power that the people could and should wield. Paine and his contemporaries were just as scathing about the venal and corrupt nature of their politicians as people are today—the difference was that they, especially Paine, had something constructive to say about the alternative to that corrupt politics."[2]

Harvey Kaye,* a political scientist and author of *Thomas Paine and the Promise of America* argues: "[Paine was] possibly the most influential writer in modern human history ... his words changed the world. His voice was essentially a voice of democratic progress."[3]

Today, there are statues of Thomas Paine in Paris and New Jersey, as well as a monument to him in New York. And twenty-first century

> **❝[Paine was] possibly the most influential writer in modern human history ... his words changed the world. His voice was essentially a voice of democratic progress.[1]❞**
>
> Harvey Kaye, quoted in Brendan O'Neill, "Who Was Thomas Paine?"

American president Barack Obama quoted Paine in his 2009 inauguration speech in reference to the economic crisis, stating:"Let it be told to the future world ... that in the depth of winter, when nothing but hope and virtue could survive ... that the city and the country, alarmed at one common danger, came forth to meet [it]."[4]

There can be no clearer example of the enduring interest in Paine and *Rights of Man*.

## Interaction

It is difficult to find contemporary schools of thought and thinkers who do not agree with Paine's broader argument. But the same cannot be said for supporters of the text's more specific proposals and assumptions—particularly regarding the representative model of democracy* and the state's role in fighting inequality and promoting the people's welfare.

One school of thought is a participatory democracy model, where the state creates institutional arenas that allow citizens to participate in the decision-making process where the issues affect the entire community. This has even extended to citizens having a say in how some government budgets are actually prioritized and spent. The city of Porto Alegre in Brazil, for example, has tried this model in recent times.

We can assume Paine would argue that direct participation, even on a local government level, is unfeasible and undesirable, even if it were practical. He would most likely claim representation enhances democracy.

With regard to the role of the state, people who follow a neoliberal doctrine, (believing the state should have a very small role in regulating both society and the economy) firmly oppose creating or continuing a welfare state.* Paine believed in a number of ideas, mainly policies of redistribution, that would not fit in with a neoliberal standpoint. These include the following:

- Providing for the poor
- Taxing property rather than consumption
- Establishing pensions for the elderly
- Securing wages
- Free education

In the present intellectual climate, democracy and individual rights are hardly contested as ideas, even from a traditionally hostile conservative viewpoint. But the experiences of countless people demonstrate the routine abuse of both. The views Paine expresses in *Rights of Man* still resonate with people who are fighting for their freedoms.

## The Continuing Debate

Dismissed by some and celebrated by others, Thomas Paine has always provoked controversy, and no clear agreement in the area of political philosophy about his status has been reached. Some contemporary commentators and scholars—among them Pauline Maier,* Joseph Ellis,* and David McCullough*—claim Paine has been overrated. Others argue the opposite: that he hasn't received the credit and attention he deserves.[5] Regardless of who is right, current debates show that *Rights of Man* occupies a very specific place in the history of political ideas.

At the end of the nineteenth century and in the first decades of the twentieth, Thomas Paine was not central to the thoughts of political theorists.[6] But American popular culture reclaimed Paine starting in the 1930s, particularly with Frank Smith's* insightful 1938 biography and the historical novel *Citizen Tom Paine* by Howard Fast* that came five years later. In 1945, American labor historian Philip S. Foner* helped return Paine to the center of discussion with his two-volume collection *The Complete Writings of Thomas Paine*.

The 1976 bicentennial of the American Revolution* sparked more academic interest in Paine and his writings. This revival continued through the 1980s, thanks in part to the 1989 bicentennial of the French Revolution.* Historians David Freeman Hawke* and Eric Foner* spearheaded this reexamination of Paine's work.

Paine and his works are still important to the history of political philosophy, but do not occupy the center of active scholarly debate. Interest in Paine's legacy is more frequently historical and biographical. Much of the literature on his life and works explores his role in three political and social contexts: the American Revolution, the Edmund Burke* controversy, and his more provocative writings on religion. Few, if any, attempts have been made to bring Paine to the forefront of current issues, a sign that current thinkers or schools of thought have little if anything to say on the matter. But their silence should not be mistaken for indifference. Paine's impact—whether overrated or celebrated—is unquestionable.

## NOTES

1   Brendan O'Neill, "Who Was Thomas Paine," BBC News, June 8, 2009, accessed February 23, 2015, http://news.bbc.co.uk/2/hi/uk_news/magazine/8089115.stm.

2   O'Neill, "Who Was Thomas Paine."

3   O'Neill, "Who Was Thomas Paine."

4   O'Neill, "Who Was Thomas Paine."

5   Jack Fruchtman, *The Political Philosophy of Thomas Paine* (Baltimore: Johns Hopkins University Press, 2009).

6   R. B. Bernstein, "Rediscovering Thomas Paine," *New York Law School Law Review* 39 (1994).

# MODULE 12
# WHERE NEXT?

## KEY POINTS

- *Rights of Man* is likely to continue to shape progressive* political views and struggles for equality.

- *Rights of Man* will, directly or indirectly, influence future debates about democracy, popular sovereignty,* political participation, the welfare state,* human rights, and social justice.

- *Rights of Man* is a seminal work because it has helped to shape world history from the eighteenth century to the present.

### Potential

Since Thomas Paine's *Rights of Man* was first circulated more than 200 years ago, people have celebrated it, contested it, burned it, and, at times, simply ignored and forgotten it. But its singular status has remained constant: it ranks as an inspirational text and suite of arguments against thinkers who want to legitimize privilege, inequality, and aristocratic rule.*

In the future, the text will most likely continue to shape debates regarding democracy, popular sovereignty, political participation, and the welfare state, along with human rights and social justice. While *Rights of Man* is now an old text, the problems it addresses still remain in modern global society. Hereditary privilege and succession,* social inequalities, and corruption continue to exist.

There is certainly room for new or existing scholars to better understand the legacy of Thomas Paine in the American, English, and French contexts, and perhaps in others too. There is also rich potential

> ❝ When it shall be said in any country in the world, my poor are happy; neither ignorance nor distress is to be found among them; my jails are empty of prisoners, my streets of beggars; the aged are not in want, the taxes are not oppressive; the rational world is my friend, because I am a friend of its happiness: When these things can be said, then may the country boast of its constitution and its government.[1] ❞
>
> Thomas Paine, *Rights of Man*

to apply his ideas to modern phenomena, such as the persistence of monarchical rule* and hereditary privilege, taxation, and economic distribution, and the scope of the welfare state.

Elementary and high-school curricula represent another important area where Paine's ideas could be further incorporated. From a young age students could benefit from a much greater exposure to his role in shaping our world. In the United States, for example, Paine is often overshadowed by the country's other "Founding Fathers,"* even though American revolutionary and statesman Benjamin Franklin* mentored Paine himself.

### Future Directions

Paine declared that human beings should govern themselves, without being subjected to dictatorial or imposed government. This idea will continue to be relevant as long as there are illegitimate rulers in the world. While the way in which people choose to govern themselves may take different forms in different societies, the idea itself will remain closely connected to Paine's notion of a self-organized society.

*Rights of Man* addressed the status of the very idea of politics itself. Rather than considering it a subject exclusive to ruling and educated elites, Paine believed political discussion should be accessible to all—precisely because politics affects everybody. According to Paine, political debate is not the privilege of any particular group or section of society, but an essential part of the everyday life of everybody who is capable of thinking about it. This idea will continue to be relevant for generations to come. As long as anyone attempts to claim the arena of politics for a specific group— specialists, an educated elite, a wealthy minority—political participation will remain a question of rights.

Universal rights* derive from the simple fact of being human and this forms the central pillar of Paine's views. This will continue to be a radical proposition, because it inevitably endorses ideas of respect, equality, and recognition, whether those claims are made between sections of a people or between a people and their government.

### Summary

For more than two centuries *Rights of Man* has been a seminal work. It influenced the reform movement* in nineteenth-century England,* the anti-slavery movement in nineteenth-century America, and anti-colonial struggles* in Africa and Asia against European powers in the twentieth century. It has also inspired many democrats,* labor activists, and religious freethinkers* around the world.

Paine made important contributions to the liberal-democratic* system of government. He influenced debates on universal individual rights, republican government,* popular sovereignty, and the welfare state. Although Paine was generally against government intrusion in the lives of its citizens, he did advocate its intervention when it came to guaranteeing social justice. This became particularly important in the twentieth century when welfare states were established, and remains important today.

Thomas Paine was a proud radical with a humble upbringing. He suffered adversity and hardship, but he survived. He was passionately committed to universal ideals and social justice. He lived through both the American\* and French Revolutions\* and had a major impact on both sides of the Atlantic subsequently. He truly was a "citizen of the world" who struggled against injustice everywhere, and the man and his work will continue to be studied, thought about, and referenced in the future.

*Rights of Man* challenged the status quo of long-established regimes and the exclusion of ordinary people from political debate. It inspired generations of reformers to take up the fight for more equal and just societies. It is a legacy Thomas Paine would surely be proud of.

## NOTES

1    Thomas Paine, *Rights of Man* (London: Collector's Library, 2004), section 2.7.

# GLOSSARY

# GLOSSARY OF TERMS

**Age of Democratic Revolution:** the period of the eighteenth century defined in part by the French and the American Revolutions.

**American Revolution:** a political upheaval of the late 1700s where 13 British colonies gained independence from the British Empire to form a new sovereign nation, the United States of America.

***Ancien régime:*** the name of the French political and social system before the Revolution of 1789. It was characterized by aristocratic rule and hereditary succession and is referred to in English as the "old regime."

**Anglican:** a member of the reformed Church of England. Thomas Paine's mother was Anglican.

**Anti-colonial struggles:** a series of violent and non-violent struggles that took place in many countries in Africa and Asia against the ruling colonial powers, including Great Britain and France.

**Aristocracy:** a form of government where power is held by the nobility. Thomas Paine argued against aristocratic rule.

**Battle of Waterloo:** a battle of June 18, 1815 where the Imperial French army was defeated, signaling the end of Emperor Napoleon's imperial rule in France.

**Bicameral legislature:** a legislative body that has two houses, chambers, or branches. Thomas Paine initially rejected this system when the United States adopted it, but later approved of it.

**Bill of Rights, The:** passed in England in 1689, it recognized a number of rights and guarantees for all Englishmen, such as freedom of speech and no cruel punishments.

**British radical movement:** a radical movement that aimed to transform British society, particularly its political system. Thomas Paine was one of the leaders in this movement.

**Chartism:** a working-class movement active between 1838 and 1848 that aimed to reform the British political system. Its name derived from the People's Charter of 1838, which proposed major reforms to make the British political system more democratic.

**Civil rights:** rights legally granted by a society to all individuals who form that society. This can be distinguished from natural rights, which, according to Paine, are the right of all human beings by virtue of their existence.

**Classical liberalism:** a political ideology that advocates limited government and the freedom of individuals (i.e. the freedom of speech, religion, markets, assembly, and press). It is likely Paine was influenced by classical liberal thinkers such as Thomas Hobbes and John Locke.

**Colonialism:** control by one country over another, generally for the purpose of economic exploitation.

**"Community of goods":** the joint ownership of goods that serve a human need.

**Conservatism:** the preference for preserving the existing laws and traditions of a society rather than advocating radical change.

**Constitutionalism:** the idea, often associated with political philosopher John Locke and the founders of the American republic, that government officials should respect all laws that limit their powers. Paine advocated this system of government.

**Cosmopolitanism:** the belief that all human beings, regardless of nationality, should struggle for universal equality.

**Declaration of Independence:** adopted on July 4, 1776, it announced that the 13 American colonies were no longer under the control of the British Empire. Thomas Paine's pamphlet *Common Sense* helped inspire the American Revolution.

**Declaration of the Rights of Man and of the Citizen:** adopted in France on August 26, 1789 by the National Assembly during the French Revolution, it identified individual rights regarding liberty, property, security, and resistance to oppression. However, various groups of society—women, for example—were not considered entitled to any of these rights.

**Deism:** the belief that reason and observation of the natural world are sufficient to prove the existence of God and that, since God created the world and then left it to its own devices, He does not exercise any control over life.

**Democrat:** a person who supports democracy or is a member of the American Democratic Party.

**Despotism:** a form of government where the ruler holds absolute power.

**Direct democracy:** a form of government where citizens are themselves the decision-makers. Thomas Paine believed that the best system for all nations was a representative democracy, a form of government where citizens elect a body of representatives who will then act in their name, rather than making public decisions directly ("direct democracy").

**East London Democratic Association**: a radical organization formed in 1837 that advocated progressive change, rather than preserving tradition.

**Enlightenment:** also known as "the Age of Reason," it was a Western intellectual movement that ran from the 1650s to the 1780s. It aimed to question tradition and religious belief, while advancing knowledge through scientific methods.

**Founding Fathers:** a sizeable group of American political leaders who took part in the American Revolution between 1765 and 1783. The seven most important figures were John Adams, Benjamin Franklin, Alexander Hamilton, John Jay, Thomas Jefferson, James Madison, and George Washington. Thomas Paine is often marginalized from this group, even though he deserves to be classified at the same level.

**Freethinker:** someone who does not rely on tradition or established beliefs in their thought.

**French Revolution (1789–99):** a period of deep political and social transformation in France that influenced the course of Western history. Thomas Paine participated in it and staunchly supported the overthrow of the old regime.

**Girondists:** one of the political factions during the French Revolution. Thomas Paine was accused of association with this group and incarcerated for one year as a penalty.

**Glorious Revolution, The, or the Revolution of 1688:** the (largely peaceful) overthrow of King James II of England and the establishment of William of Orange and his wife Mary as joint monarchs in his place. Edmund Burke argued that this revolution had achieved a stable balance between the monarchy and the people, and any further revolution would be wrong.

**Hereditary succession:** the system whereby a member of a ruler's family takes over after their death.

**Inalienable:** if a right is inalienable, it cannot be taken away or transferred to another person.

**Industrial revolution:** a period of rapid economic and social change from an agrarian economy to one dominated by machines and industry. The Industrial Revolution began in England in the eighteenth century and later spread to Western Europe and the United States. Thomas Paine was deeply concerned by the social inequalities, unemployment, and poverty caused by the industrial economy.

**International arbitration:** the process in which a mediating body (such as the United Nations) resolves international disputes.

**Jeffersonian democracy movement:** an American political movement that existed between the 1790s and the 1820s. It was named in honor of Thomas Jefferson and represented the principles of republicanism, civic duty, and equality of opportunity. It relied heavily on the ideas of Thomas Paine, and particularly those written in *Rights of Man*.

**Liberal democracy:** a system of government in which elected representatives who hold power are limited by a constitution that emphasizes the protection of individual rights and equality in accordance with the law.

**Libertarian:** the belief that a government should be reduced to the minimum necessary to protect the liberty of the state's citizens.

**Loyalists:** American colonists who were loyal to the British monarchy and opposed the American Revolution.

**Magna Carta:** an English charter originally issued in Latin in the year 1215 by King John. It proclaimed certain liberties to the king's subjects and placed limits on the king's power. Edmund Burke was in favor of safeguarding traditional English laws and structures such as the Magna Carta.

**Monarchy:** a form of government where supremacy lies with a single, usually hereditary, figure, such as a king or queen. Paine opposed aristocratic rule and hereditary succession.

**National Convention:** an institution incorporating both the constitutional and legislative assembly of France during the French Revolution. Thomas Paine became a member in 1791.

**Nationalism:** the sense of loyalty to one's country or nation.

**Nationalization:** the process of making something that is private public under government or state control.

**Natural law:** the laws derived from nature to which humanity is bound, as opposed to those from constitutional law.

**Natural rights:** those rights to which all human beings are entitled by virtue of their existence.

**Neoliberalism:** the belief that the state should have a very minimal role in the regulation of both society and the economy. Neoliberalism opposes Paine's idea that the main role of government is to promote social justice.

**New World:** the Western hemisphere, particularly the Americas, and some islands in the Atlantic and Pacific oceans. Paine left for the "New World" at the age of 37 with an invitation from the great American statesman Benjamin Franklin.

**Oligarchy:** a form of government in which power is confined to a few persons or families. Also, the body of persons composing such a government.

**Painite:** a follower of Thomas Paine.

**Participatory democracy:** a political system with the emphasis on all citizens, rather than just elected representatives, taking part in the political decision making process.

**Plebeian:** a person not of noble or privileged rank; a commoner.

**Popular sovereignty:** the principle that by electing representatives, the general population gives consent to the authority of the government. Thomas Paine contributed to our modern-day understanding of this term.

**Progressive:** someone who advocates change or improvement rather than seeking to preserve the traditional system.

**Progressive taxation:** the system of taxation whereby the percentage of tax payable increases in relation to income received.

**Quaker:** a Christian sect founded by George Fox, an English religious leader, in about 1650. Thomas Paine's father was a Quaker.

**Reform Bill:** passed into law as the Great Reform Act in 1832, it effectively empowered the middle class. The ideas of Thomas Paine inspired progressive political, economic, and social reform in Britain.

**Reform movement:** a political movement that campaigned for the transformation of British society, particularly the political system, during the late eighteenth and early nineteenth century.

**Representation of the People Act:** an 1832 Act of Parliament that changed the electoral system of England and Wales. In particular, it extended the right to vote to more of the population.

**Representative democracy:** a form of government in which citizens, rather than making public decisions directly ("direct democracy"), elect a body of representatives who will then act in their name. Paine advocated this system.

**Republican government:** one in which the head of the government is not selected by heredity but by other means, most commonly through elections.

**Republicanism:** a form of government characterized by the active role citizens play and the establishment of institutions that aim to combat corruption and promote the rule of law. Most importantly, the head of the government is not selected by rules of heredity but by other means, most commonly through elections. Thomas Paine was an advocate of republicanism.

**Seditious libel:** the punishable offense of criticizing or defaming the government.

**Socialism:** the belief that society should be organized in such a way that the methods of production, distribution, and exchange are owned and regulated by the community as a whole, rather than by the select few. Many subsequent socialists were inspired by Thomas Paine's radical ideas.

**Stay-maker:** a person skilled in corsetry and dressmaking.

**Terror, The:** the term used to refer to the period of the French Revolution between September 1793 and July 1794 that was marked by violence and executions due to conflicts between two rival factions, the Girondists and the Jacobins.

**Thirteen Colonies:** the American territories that declared their independence from Britain in 1776. Thomas Paine inspired them with his work *Common Sense*, in which he argued that the time had come for a revolution against a corrupt and abusive British monarchy.

**Universal rights:** the basic rights to which all humans are entitled. For Paine, this was life, liberty, and the pursuit of happiness.

**Universal suffrage:** the right to vote for all adult citizens. In Paine's time the demands for universal suffrage applied to qualifying men only.

**Welfare state:** a model of government in which the state plays a central role in promoting and securing the economic and social well-being of its citizens by actively participating in the functioning of the economy. The ideas of Thomas Paine contributed to laying the foundations for the modern welfare state.

# PEOPLE MENTIONED IN THE TEXT

**Jeremy Bentham (1748–1832)** was a British jurist, philosopher, and social reformer. He advocated the abolition of slavery and the death penalty, equal rights for women, and the separation of church and state.

**John Brown (1800–59)** was a white American abolitionist who defended armed revolt as the only way to do away with slavery in the United States.

**Edmund Burke (1729–97)** was an Irish statesman, political thinker, and orator, who wrote *Reflections on the Revolution in France*. Well known for his speeches and practical writings, he served as a member of parliament for the Whig Party in Great Britain. *Rights of Man* was a direct response to Burke's view that the monarchy should be safeguarded against revolt.

**Gregory Claeys** is professor of the history of political thought at Royal Holloway, University of London.

**William Cobbett (1763–1835)** was a British political activist, journalist, and farmer. Formerly a loyalist, he joined the radical movement and campaigned alongside Thomas Paine for the reform of Parliament and other progressive causes.

**Eugene "Gene" Victor Debs (1855–1926)** was an American socialist and union leader, and one of the founders of the Industrial Workers of the World, a twentieth-century international workers' union.

**Joseph John Ellis (b. 1943)** is an American historian whose work centers on the lives of the founders of the United States of America.

**Howard Melvin Fast (1914–2003)** was an American television writer and novelist. He published the book *Citizen Thomas Paine*.

**Eric Foner (b. 1943)** is a renowned American historian and a professor of history at Columbia University. He has published numerous works on American history, including *Tom Paine and Revolutionary America*.

**Philip Sheldon Foner (1910–94)** was an American Marxist labor historian and teacher, best known for his 10-volume *History of the Labor Movement in the United States* and *The Life and Writings of Frederick Douglass*.

**Benjamin Franklin (1706–90)** was one of the most important American figures in the struggle for colonial independence. Franklin wrote Paine a generous letter of introduction that allowed him to enter political circles upon his arrival in Pennsylvania in 1774.

**William Godwin (1756–1836)** was an English political philosopher, journalist, and novelist. He argued that Thomas Paine's view was not radical enough because he did not attack ownership of private property.

**George Julian Harney (1817–97)** was an important British Chartist leader and journalist.

**David Freeman Hawke (1924–99)** was an American historian whose work focused on the history of the United States from colonial times to the twentieth century. He wrote a book on Paine in 1992.

**Christopher Hitchens (1949–2011)** was a British-American author and journalist who wrote a biography of Paine's *Rights of Man*.

**Thomas Hobbes (1588–1679)** was an English political philosopher, best known today for his political commentary *Leviathan*.

**Cheryl Hudson** is a fellow at the Rothermere American Institute at Oxford University.

**Robert Green Ingersoll (1833–99)** was an American politician who was well known for his speeches during what is now known as the "Golden Age of Freethought." He was influenced by the ideas of Thomas Paine.

**Harvey Kaye** is a professor of democracy and justice studies at the University of Wisconsin, Green Bay.

**Yuval Levin** is a political scientist, editor of US political affairs magazine *National Affairs,* and author of *The Great Debate: Edmund Burke, Thomas Paine, and the Birth of Left and Right*.

**Abraham Lincoln (1809–65)** was president of the United States from 1861 until his assassination in 1865. He led the country through the Civil War and abolished slavery.

**John Locke (1632–1704)** was an English philosopher, the father of classical liberalism★, and one of the most influential thinkers of the Enlightenment movement. His most influential work is *Two Treatises on Government*.

**Pauline Alice Maier (1938–2013)** was a historian of the American Revolution who taught at the Massachusetts Institute of Technology (MIT).

**David Gaub McCullough (b. 1933)** is an American author, historian, and lecturer who graduated from Yale University. He has twice won the Pulitzer Prize and the National Book Award.

**Charles-Louis de Secondat, Baron de La Brède et de Montesquieu (1689–1755)** was a French political thinker who became widely known for his theory of separation of powers.

**Barack Obama (b. 1961)** has been the president of the United States since 2009. He is the first African American president in American history.

**James Bronterre O'Brien (1805–64)** was an Irish Chartist leader and journalist who played an important role in publicizing reformist ideas in Britain.

**Robert Owen (1771–1858)** was one of the most important socialist thinkers and was responsible for the foundation of the Cooperative movement. He focused on fair compensation for labor rather than on debates regarding natural rights.

**Jean-Jacques Rousseau (1712–78)** was a Genevan political philosopher who greatly influenced the French Revolution. His 1762 work *On the Social Contract* confirmed him as one of the greatest modern thinkers.

**Frank Smith** was the author of *Thomas Paine: Liberator*, published in 1938.

**Thomas Spence (1750–1814)** was an English radical and an advocate of the common ownership of land. He was deeply influenced by Thomas Paine.

**Edward Palmer (E. P.) Thompson (1924–93)** was a British historian best known for his pioneering studies on the history of the working class.

**Voltaire (François-Marie Arouet) (1694–1778)** was a French philosopher, writer, and historian. He was famous for his defense of basic freedoms and his views may well have influenced Thomas Paine.

**Walter "Walt" Whitman (1819–92)** was an American poet, essayist, and journalist who became influential for his innovative practice of "free verse." Among his most well-known books is the poetry collection *Leaves of Grass*. He wrote pieces on Thomas Paine, and contributed to reviving his legacy.

**Frances "Fanny" Wright (1795–1852)** was a Scottish-born American social reformer, abolitionist, writer, and lecturer. In 1825 she founded the Nashoba Commune in order to prepare slaves for freedom.

# WORKS CITED

# WORKS CITED

Aldridge, Alfred Owen. *Thomas Paine's American Ideology*. Newark: University of Delaware Press, 1984.

Ayer, A. J. *Thomas Paine*. Chicago: University of Chicago Press, 1988.

Bernstein, R. B. "Rediscovering Thomas Paine." *New York Law School Law Review* 39 (1994): 873–929.

Brown, Nat. "Edmund Burke v. Thomas Paine." *National Review*, December 3, 2013. Accessed February 23, 2015. http://www.nationalreview.com/article/365296/edmund-burke-v-thomas-paine-nat-brown.

Burke, Edmund. *Reflections on the Revolution in France*. Vol. 24, part 3 of *The Harvard Classics*. New York: P. F. Collier & Son, 1909–14.

Claeys, Gregory. *Thomas Paine: Social and Political Thought*. Boston: Unwin Hyman, 1989.

Foner, Eric. *Tom Paine and Revolutionary America*. London: Oxford University Press, 1976.

Fruchtman, Jack. *The Political Philosophy of Thomas Paine*. Baltimore: Johns Hopkins University Press, 2009.

"'Common Sense' and its Meaning Today by Jack Fruchtman." The Thomas Paine National Historical Association and the Thomas Paine Foundation, January 26, 2001. Accessed February 23, 2015. http://thomaspaine.org/aboutpaine/common-sense-and-its-meaning-today-by-jack-fruchtman.html.

Goodwin, Albert. *The Friends of Liberty: The English Democratic Movement in the Age of the French Revolution*. London: Hutchinson, 1979.

Hitchens, Christopher. *Thomas Paine's* Rights of Man*: A Biography*. New York: Grove Press, 2006.

Kaye, Harvey J. *Thomas Paine: Firebrand of the Revolution*. New York: Oxford University Press, 2000.

*Thomas Paine and the Promise of America*. New York: Hill and Wang, 2005.

Locke, John. *Two Treatises of Government and A Letter Concerning Toleration*. New Haven and London: Yale University Press, 2003.

O'Neill, Brendan. "Who Was Thomas Paine." BBC News, June 8, 2009. Accessed February 23, 2015. http://news.bbc.co.uk/2/hi/uk_news/magazine/8089115.stm.

Paine, Thomas. *Rights of Man*. London: Collector's Library of Essential Thinkers, 2004.

*The Thomas Paine Reader*. Edited by Michael Foot and Isaac Kramnick. Harmondsworth: Penguin, 1987.

Philp, Mark. *Paine*. Oxford: Oxford University Press, 1989.

# THE MACAT LIBRARY
# BY DISCIPLINE

## AFRICANA STUDIES

Chinua Achebe's *An Image of Africa: Racism in Conrad's Heart of Darkness*
W. E. B. Du Bois's *The Souls of Black Folk*
Zora Neale Huston's *Characteristics of Negro Expression*
Martin Luther King Jr's *Why We Can't Wait*
Toni Morrison's *Playing in the Dark: Whiteness in the American Literary Imagination*

## ANTHROPOLOGY

Arjun Appadurai's *Modernity at Large: Cultural Dimensions of Globalisation*
Philippe Ariès's *Centuries of Childhood*
Franz Boas's *Race, Language and Culture*
Kim Chan & Renée Mauborgne's *Blue Ocean Strategy*
Jared Diamond's *Guns, Germs & Steel: the Fate of Human Societies*
Jared Diamond's *Collapse: How Societies Choose to Fail or Survive*
E. E. Evans-Pritchard's *Witchcraft, Oracles and Magic Among the Azande*
James Ferguson's *The Anti-Politics Machine*
Clifford Geertz's *The Interpretation of Cultures*
David Graeber's *Debt: the First 5000 Years*
Karen Ho's *Liquidated: An Ethnography of Wall Street*
Geert Hofstede's *Culture's Consequences: Comparing Values, Behaviors, Institutes and Organizations across Nations*
Claude Lévi-Strauss's *Structural Anthropology*
Jay Macleod's *Ain't No Makin' It: Aspirations and Attainment in a Low-Income Neighborhood*
Saba Mahmood's *The Politics of Piety: The Islamic Revival and the Feminist Subject*
Marcel Mauss's *The Gift*

## BUSINESS

Jean Lave & Etienne Wenger's *Situated Learning*
Theodore Levitt's *Marketing Myopia*
Burton G. Malkiel's *A Random Walk Down Wall Street*
Douglas McGregor's *The Human Side of Enterprise*
Michael Porter's *Competitive Strategy: Creating and Sustaining Superior Performance*
John Kotter's *Leading Change*
C. K. Prahalad & Gary Hamel's *The Core Competence of the Corporation*

## CRIMINOLOGY

Michelle Alexander's *The New Jim Crow: Mass Incarceration in the Age of Colorblindness*
Michael R. Gottfredson & Travis Hirschi's *A General Theory of Crime*
Richard Herrnstein & Charles A. Murray's *The Bell Curve: Intelligence and Class Structure in American Life*
Elizabeth Loftus's *Eyewitness Testimony*
Jay Macleod's *Ain't No Makin' It: Aspirations and Attainment in a Low-Income Neighborhood*
Philip Zimbardo's *The Lucifer Effect*

## ECONOMICS

Janet Abu-Lughod's *Before European Hegemony*
Ha-Joon Chang's *Kicking Away the Ladder*
David Brion Davis's *The Problem of Slavery in the Age of Revolution*
Milton Friedman's *The Role of Monetary Policy*
Milton Friedman's *Capitalism and Freedom*
David Graeber's *Debt: the First 5000 Years*
Friedrich Hayek's *The Road to Serfdom*
Karen Ho's *Liquidated: An Ethnography of Wall Street*

John Maynard Keynes's *The General Theory of Employment, Interest and Money*
Charles P. Kindleberger's *Manias, Panics and Crashes*
Robert Lucas's *Why Doesn't Capital Flow from Rich to Poor Countries?*
Burton G. Malkiel's *A Random Walk Down Wall Street*
Thomas Robert Malthus's *An Essay on the Principle of Population*
Karl Marx's *Capital*
Thomas Piketty's *Capital in the Twenty-First Century*
Amartya Sen's *Development as Freedom*
Adam Smith's *The Wealth of Nations*
Nassim Nicholas Taleb's *The Black Swan: The Impact of the Highly Improbable*
Amos Tversky's & Daniel Kahneman's *Judgment under Uncertainty: Heuristics and Biases*
Mahbub Ul Haq's *Reflections on Human Development*
Max Weber's *The Protestant Ethic and the Spirit of Capitalism*

## FEMINISM AND GENDER STUDIES

Judith Butler's *Gender Trouble*
Simone De Beauvoir's *The Second Sex*
Michel Foucault's *History of Sexuality*
Betty Friedan's *The Feminine Mystique*
Saba Mahmood's *The Politics of Piety: The Islamic Revival and the Feminist Subject*
Joan Wallach Scott's *Gender and the Politics of History*
Mary Wollstonecraft's *A Vindication of the Rights of Women*
Virginia Woolf's *A Room of One's Own*

## GEOGRAPHY

The Brundtland Report's *Our Common Future*
Rachel Carson's *Silent Spring*
Charles Darwin's *On the Origin of Species*
James Ferguson's *The Anti-Politics Machine*
Jane Jacobs's *The Death and Life of Great American Cities*
James Lovelock's *Gaia: A New Look at Life on Earth*
Amartya Sen's *Development as Freedom*
Mathis Wackernagel & William Rees's *Our Ecological Footprint*

## HISTORY

Janet Abu-Lughod's *Before European Hegemony*
Benedict Anderson's *Imagined Communities*
Bernard Bailyn's *The Ideological Origins of the American Revolution*
Hanna Batatu's *The Old Social Classes And The Revolutionary Movements Of Iraq*
Christopher Browning's *Ordinary Men: Reserve Police Batallion 101 and the Final Solution in Poland*
Edmund Burke's *Reflections on the Revolution in France*
William Cronon's *Nature's Metropolis: Chicago And The Great West*
Alfred W. Crosby's *The Columbian Exchange*
Hamid Dabashi's *Iran: A People Interrupted*
David Brion Davis's *The Problem of Slavery in the Age of Revolution*
Nathalie Zemon Davis's *The Return of Martin Guerre*
Jared Diamond's *Guns, Germs & Steel: the Fate of Human Societies*
Frank Dikotter's *Mao's Great Famine*
John W Dower's *War Without Mercy: Race And Power In The Pacific War*
W. E. B. Du Bois's *The Souls of Black Folk*
Richard J. Evans's *In Defence of History*
Lucien Febvre's *The Problem of Unbelief in the 16th Century*
Sheila Fitzpatrick's *Everyday Stalinism*

Eric Foner's *Reconstruction: America's Unfinished Revolution, 1863-1877*
Michel Foucault's *Discipline and Punish*
Michel Foucault's *History of Sexuality*
Francis Fukuyama's *The End of History and the Last Man*
John Lewis Gaddis's *We Now Know: Rethinking Cold War History*
Ernest Gellner's *Nations and Nationalism*
Eugene Genovese's *Roll, Jordan, Roll: The World the Slaves Made*
Carlo Ginzburg's *The Night Battles*
Daniel Goldhagen's *Hitler's Willing Executioners*
Jack Goldstone's *Revolution and Rebellion in the Early Modern World*
Antonio Gramsci's *The Prison Notebooks*
Alexander Hamilton, John Jay & James Madison's *The Federalist Papers*
Christopher Hill's *The World Turned Upside Down*
Carole Hillenbrand's *The Crusades: Islamic Perspectives*
Thomas Hobbes's *Leviathan*
Eric Hobsbawm's *The Age Of Revolution*
John A. Hobson's *Imperialism: A Study*
Albert Hourani's *History of the Arab Peoples*
Samuel P. Huntington's *The Clash of Civilizations and the Remaking of World Order*
C. L. R. James's *The Black Jacobins*
Tony Judt's *Postwar: A History of Europe Since 1945*
Ernst Kantorowicz's *The King's Two Bodies: A Study in Medieval Political Theology*
Paul Kennedy's *The Rise and Fall of the Great Powers*
Ian Kershaw's *The "Hitler Myth": Image and Reality in the Third Reich*
John Maynard Keynes's *The General Theory of Employment, Interest and Money*
Charles P. Kindleberger's *Manias, Panics and Crashes*
Martin Luther King Jr's *Why We Can't Wait*
Henry Kissinger's *World Order: Reflections on the Character of Nations and the Course of History*
Thomas Kuhn's *The Structure of Scientific Revolutions*
Georges Lefebvre's *The Coming of the French Revolution*
John Locke's *Two Treatises of Government*
Niccolò Machiavelli's *The Prince*
Thomas Robert Malthus's *An Essay on the Principle of Population*
Mahmood Mamdani's *Citizen and Subject: Contemporary Africa And The Legacy Of Late Colonialism*
Karl Marx's *Capital*
Stanley Milgram's *Obedience to Authority*
John Stuart Mill's *On Liberty*
Thomas Paine's *Common Sense*
Thomas Paine's *Rights of Man*
Geoffrey Parker's *Global Crisis: War, Climate Change and Catastrophe in the Seventeenth Century*
Jonathan Riley-Smith's *The First Crusade and the Idea of Crusading*
Jean-Jacques Rousseau's *The Social Contract*
Joan Wallach Scott's *Gender and the Politics of History*
Theda Skocpol's *States and Social Revolutions*
Adam Smith's *The Wealth of Nations*
Timothy Snyder's *Bloodlands: Europe Between Hitler and Stalin*
Sun Tzu's *The Art of War*
Keith Thomas's *Religion and the Decline of Magic*
Thucydides's *The History of the Peloponnesian War*
Frederick Jackson Turner's *The Significance of the Frontier in American History*
Odd Arne Westad's *The Global Cold War: Third World Interventions And The Making Of Our Times*

## LITERATURE

Chinua Achebe's *An Image of Africa: Racism in Conrad's Heart of Darkness*
Roland Barthes's *Mythologies*
Homi K. Bhabha's *The Location of Culture*
Judith Butler's *Gender Trouble*
Simone De Beauvoir's *The Second Sex*
Ferdinand De Saussure's *Course in General Linguistics*
T. S. Eliot's *The Sacred Wood: Essays on Poetry and Criticism*
Zora Neale Huston's *Characteristics of Negro Expression*
Toni Morrison's *Playing in the Dark: Whiteness in the American Literary Imagination*
Edward Said's *Orientalism*
Gayatri Chakravorty Spivak's *Can the Subaltern Speak?*
Mary Wollstonecraft's *A Vindication of the Rights of Women*
Virginia Woolf's *A Room of One's Own*

## PHILOSOPHY

Elizabeth Anscombe's *Modern Moral Philosophy*
Hannah Arendt's *The Human Condition*
Aristotle's *Metaphysics*
Aristotle's *Nicomachean Ethics*
Edmund Gettier's *Is Justified True Belief Knowledge?*
Georg Wilhelm Friedrich Hegel's *Phenomenology of Spirit*
David Hume's *Dialogues Concerning Natural Religion*
David Hume's *The Enquiry for Human Understanding*
Immanuel Kant's *Religion within the Boundaries of Mere Reason*
Immanuel Kant's *Critique of Pure Reason*
Søren Kierkegaard's *The Sickness Unto Death*
Søren Kierkegaard's *Fear and Trembling*
C. S. Lewis's *The Abolition of Man*
Alasdair MacIntyre's *After Virtue*
Marcus Aurelius's *Meditations*
Friedrich Nietzsche's *On the Genealogy of Morality*
Friedrich Nietzsche's *Beyond Good and Evil*
Plato's *Republic*
Plato's *Symposium*
Jean-Jacques Rousseau's *The Social Contract*
Gilbert Ryle's *The Concept of Mind*
Baruch Spinoza's *Ethics*
Sun Tzu's *The Art of War*
Ludwig Wittgenstein's *Philosophical Investigations*

## POLITICS

Benedict Anderson's *Imagined Communities*
Aristotle's *Politics*
Bernard Bailyn's *The Ideological Origins of the American Revolution*
Edmund Burke's *Reflections on the Revolution in France*
John C. Calhoun's *A Disquisition on Government*
Ha-Joon Chang's *Kicking Away the Ladder*
Hamid Dabashi's *Iran: A People Interrupted*
Hamid Dabashi's *Theology of Discontent: The Ideological Foundation of the Islamic Revolution in Iran*
Robert Dahl's *Democracy and its Critics*
Robert Dahl's *Who Governs?*
David Brion Davis's *The Problem of Slavery in the Age of Revolution*

Alexis De Tocqueville's *Democracy in America*
James Ferguson's *The Anti-Politics Machine*
Frank Dikotter's *Mao's Great Famine*
Sheila Fitzpatrick's *Everyday Stalinism*
Eric Foner's *Reconstruction: America's Unfinished Revolution, 1863-1877*
Milton Friedman's *Capitalism and Freedom*
Francis Fukuyama's *The End of History and the Last Man*
John Lewis Gaddis's *We Now Know: Rethinking Cold War History*
Ernest Gellner's *Nations and Nationalism*
David Graeber's *Debt: the First 5000 Years*
Antonio Gramsci's *The Prison Notebooks*
Alexander Hamilton, John Jay & James Madison's *The Federalist Papers*
Friedrich Hayek's *The Road to Serfdom*
Christopher Hill's *The World Turned Upside Down*
Thomas Hobbes's *Leviathan*
John A. Hobson's *Imperialism: A Study*
Samuel P. Huntington's *The Clash of Civilizations and the Remaking of World Order*
Tony Judt's *Postwar: A History of Europe Since 1945*
David C. Kang's *China Rising: Peace, Power and Order in East Asia*
Paul Kennedy's *The Rise and Fall of Great Powers*
Robert Keohane's *After Hegemony*
Martin Luther King Jr.'s *Why We Can't Wait*
Henry Kissinger's *World Order: Reflections on the Character of Nations and the Course of History*
John Locke's *Two Treatises of Government*
Niccolò Machiavelli's *The Prince*
Thomas Robert Malthus's *An Essay on the Principle of Population*
Mahmood Mamdani's *Citizen and Subject: Contemporary Africa And The Legacy Of Late Colonialism*
Karl Marx's *Capital*
John Stuart Mill's *On Liberty*
John Stuart Mill's *Utilitarianism*
Hans Morgenthau's *Politics Among Nations*
Thomas Paine's *Common Sense*
Thomas Paine's *Rights of Man*
Thomas Piketty's *Capital in the Twenty-First Century*
Robert D. Putman's *Bowling Alone*
John Rawls's *Theory of Justice*
Jean-Jacques Rousseau's *The Social Contract*
Theda Skocpol's *States and Social Revolutions*
Adam Smith's *The Wealth of Nations*
Sun Tzu's *The Art of War*
Henry David Thoreau's *Civil Disobedience*
Thucydides's *The History of the Peloponnesian War*
Kenneth Waltz's *Theory of International Politics*
Max Weber's *Politics as a Vocation*
Odd Arne Westad's *The Global Cold War: Third World Interventions And The Making Of Our Times*

## POSTCOLONIAL STUDIES

Roland Barthes's *Mythologies*
Frantz Fanon's *Black Skin, White Masks*
Homi K. Bhabha's *The Location of Culture*
Gustavo Gutiérrez's *A Theology of Liberation*
Edward Said's *Orientalism*
Gayatri Chakravorty Spivak's *Can the Subaltern Speak?*

## PSYCHOLOGY

Gordon Allport's *The Nature of Prejudice*
Alan Baddeley & Graham Hitch's *Aggression: A Social Learning Analysis*
Albert Bandura's *Aggression: A Social Learning Analysis*
Leon Festinger's *A Theory of Cognitive Dissonance*
Sigmund Freud's *The Interpretation of Dreams*
Betty Friedan's *The Feminine Mystique*
Michael R. Gottfredson & Travis Hirschi's *A General Theory of Crime*
Eric Hoffer's *The True Believer: Thoughts on the Nature of Mass Movements*
William James's *Principles of Psychology*
Elizabeth Loftus's *Eyewitness Testimony*
A. H. Maslow's *A Theory of Human Motivation*
Stanley Milgram's *Obedience to Authority*
Steven Pinker's *The Better Angels of Our Nature*
Oliver Sacks's *The Man Who Mistook His Wife For a Hat*
Richard Thaler & Cass Sunstein's *Nudge: Improving Decisions About Health, Wealth and Happiness*
Amos Tversky's *Judgment under Uncertainty: Heuristics and Biases*
Philip Zimbardo's *The Lucifer Effect*

## SCIENCE

Rachel Carson's *Silent Spring*
William Cronon's *Nature's Metropolis: Chicago And The Great West*
Alfred W. Crosby's *The Columbian Exchange*
Charles Darwin's *On the Origin of Species*
Richard Dawkin's *The Selfish Gene*
Thomas Kuhn's *The Structure of Scientific Revolutions*
Geoffrey Parker's *Global Crisis: War, Climate Change and Catastrophe in the Seventeenth Century*
Mathis Wackernagel & William Rees's *Our Ecological Footprint*

## SOCIOLOGY

Michelle Alexander's *The New Jim Crow: Mass Incarceration in the Age of Colorblindness*
Gordon Allport's *The Nature of Prejudice*
Albert Bandura's *Aggression: A Social Learning Analysis*
Hanna Batatu's *The Old Social Classes And The Revolutionary Movements Of Iraq*
Ha-Joon Chang's *Kicking Away the Ladder*
W. E. B. Du Bois's *The Souls of Black Folk*
Émile Durkheim's *On Suicide*
Frantz Fanon's *Black Skin, White Masks*
Frantz Fanon's *The Wretched of the Earth*
Eric Foner's *Reconstruction: America's Unfinished Revolution, 1863-1877*
Eugene Genovese's *Roll, Jordan, Roll: The World the Slaves Made*
Jack Goldstone's *Revolution and Rebellion in the Early Modern World*
Antonio Gramsci's *The Prison Notebooks*
Richard Herrnstein & Charles A Murray's *The Bell Curve: Intelligence and Class Structure in American Life*
Eric Hoffer's *The True Believer: Thoughts on the Nature of Mass Movements*
Jane Jacobs's *The Death and Life of Great American Cities*
Robert Lucas's *Why Doesn't Capital Flow from Rich to Poor Countries?*
Jay Macleod's *Ain't No Makin' It: Aspirations and Attainment in a Low Income Neighborhood*
Elaine May's *Homeward Bound: American Families in the Cold War Era*
Douglas McGregor's *The Human Side of Enterprise*
C. Wright Mills's *The Sociological Imagination*

Thomas Piketty's *Capital in the Twenty-First Century*
Robert D. Putman's *Bowling Alone*
David Riesman's *The Lonely Crowd: A Study of the Changing American Character*
Edward Said's *Orientalism*
Joan Wallach Scott's *Gender and the Politics of History*
Theda Skocpol's *States and Social Revolutions*
Max Weber's *The Protestant Ethic and the Spirit of Capitalism*

## THEOLOGY

Augustine's *Confessions*
Benedict's *Rule of St Benedict*
Gustavo Gutiérrez's *A Theology of Liberation*
Carole Hillenbrand's *The Crusades: Islamic Perspectives*
David Hume's *Dialogues Concerning Natural Religion*
Immanuel Kant's *Religion within the Boundaries of Mere Reason*
Ernst Kantorowicz's *The King's Two Bodies: A Study in Medieval Political Theology*
Søren Kierkegaard's *The Sickness Unto Death*
C. S. Lewis's *The Abolition of Man*
Saba Mahmood's *The Politics of Piety: The Islamic Revival and the Feminist Subject*
Baruch Spinoza's *Ethics*
Keith Thomas's *Religion and the Decline of Magic*

## COMING SOON

Chris Argyris's *The Individual and the Organisation*
Seyla Benhabib's *The Rights of Others*
Walter Benjamin's *The Work Of Art in the Age of Mechanical Reproduction*
John Berger's *Ways of Seeing*
Pierre Bourdieu's *Outline of a Theory of Practice*
Mary Douglas's *Purity and Danger*
Roland Dworkin's *Taking Rights Seriously*
James G. March's *Exploration and Exploitation in Organisational Learning*
Ikujiro Nonaka's *A Dynamic Theory of Organizational Knowledge Creation*
Griselda Pollock's *Vision and Difference*
Amartya Sen's *Inequality Re-Examined*
Susan Sontag's *On Photography*
Yasser Tabbaa's *The Transformation of Islamic Art*
Ludwig von Mises's *Theory of Money and Credit*